THE
PHYSICAL
SIDE OF
BEING
SPIRITUAL

By the same author

LOVE IS NOW
HANDBOOK FOR SPIRITUAL SURVIVAL
LET'S QUIT FIGHTING ABOUT THE HOLY SPIRIT

THE
PHYSICAL
SIDE OF
BEING
SPIRITUAL

Peter E. Gillquist

ZONDERVAN
PUBLISHING HOUSE   OF THE ZONDERVAN CORPORATION
GRAND RAPIDS, MICHIGAN 49506

THE PHYSICAL SIDE OF BEING SPIRITUAL
© 1979 by The Zondervan Corporation
Grand Rapids, Michigan

Library of Congress Cataloging in Publication Data
Gillquist, Peter E
    The physical side of being spiritual.

    1. Theology, Doctrinal—Popular works. 2. Evangelicalism. I. Title.
BT77.G48   230   79-12096
ISBN 0-310-36950-9

Printed in the United States of America

For MARILYN
for me God's best
from all sides

CONTENTS

PREFACE

Ever since writing *Love Is Now* back in 1970, I have been asked, "We know what you believe about the grace of God, how God accepts you just as you are, and how He absolutely forgives your sins because of His unchanging love. But what do you believe about human accountability, obedience, and faithfulness?"

This book answers that question. But it goes beyond simply holding a biblical *view* of human responsibility or grasping the truth. For when we believe and obey God, it is far more than a mental attitude or a spiritual agreement. It also has to do with physically carrying out what God tells us to do. And such obedience is connected with worship, good (not dead) works, and being accountable to one another in the body of Christ.

Frankly, I'm out to evangelize evangelicals! I am writing to say that confessing a belief in Jesus Christ and having a *personal* relationship with Him is only a fraction of all that our Lord Jesus Christ meant when He said, "Unless one is born again, he cannot see the Kingdom of God" (John 3:3). Justification by faith is the marvelous beginning of the relationship, but the faith itself includes far more.

Honestly, it is time for us to get off our pop-evangelicalism, our schemes of spiritual shortcuts, and back into the wholeness of the historic Christian faith. I am calling for community instead of mere individualism, good deeds instead of just good thoughts, care instead of only prayer, and a worship which goes far beyond a personal quiet time—or being a congregation of *spectators*.

I am writing, then, to the growing numbers of moderns who have lapsed towards a private, invisible, mental Christianity, who are trying to worship, communicate with, and enthusiastically serve their very personal God—and who know they are not succeeding.

PETER E. GILLQUIST
Isla Vista, California

ACKNOWLEDGMENTS

A grateful word of thanks goes to several people who served as idea reservoirs for this book, and, some of them as most helpful editors for the final manuscript: Jack Sparks, Richard Ballew, and Jon Braun and their students at the Academy of Orthodox Theology; Ken Berven, Gordon Walker, Bill Blythe, Dale Autrey, and my other colleagues on the Council of the Evangelical Orthodox Church; Thomas Howard of Gordon College; and to Martin Marty of the University of Chicago School of Divinity, and Robert Webber of Wheaton College for some greatly encouraging personal conversations. Finally, to Linda Wallace, Bonnie Franzen, Luanne Dunaway, and Shirley Dillon for their unselfish availability as typists for this manuscript, and to Ron and Marilyn Elder for a last-minute read-through, I offer my sincere thanks.

And God saw all that He had made, and behold, it was very good.

Moses

1

———— HOW ————
GOOD TO BE PHYSICAL

As did some of our forebears in other times and other places, we in the twentieth century have to get it through our heads that it is not bad to be physical. Just as the ancient Greeks taught the inherent evil of matter, so it seems that we have once again flirted with this erroneous concept, thinking it far more noble to be without bodies than to be with them. We have become so attuned to being "spiritual creatures" that we have forgotten the place of a healthy, godly appreciation for being physical people in a created material setting. Mark it well: it is *good* to be physical.

In our zeal to be spiritual have we become a generation of "evangelical Essenes"? The current craze for Christian sex books is a symptom of our state of being. Have not the people of God known for millenniums of the ways of a man with a maid? Certainly the knowledge of such matters has not been limited to natural men, with we who are spiritual making such discoveries only recently.

What can we learn from the ready market for this new cry for human intimacy on the part of the regenerate? That Saran-wrapped greetings at the front door or candlelight parties under the dining room table help bring new sizzle to a tuckered-out marriage? I mean, is that the way people who belong to God are really supposed to get things on? Or is the massive response to these secret schemes saying to us that we've had a horrible view of our physical bodies, and that now it's time to step out of our closets of shameful modesty and, by acting a bit crazy, admit to each other that sex is kind of fun after all?

Or let us take a totally different symptom of our problem: today's "churchless Christianity." In one generation, we have gone all the way from the view that "if you belong to a church, of course you are a Christian" to "you don't need the visible, physical church; all you need is Jesus." Which really is the eye saying to the hand, "I have no need of you."[1]

The trend today is to find one's own private spiritual mentor. We turn on the television and tune in our favorite speaker or talk show-host evangelist. Through him we "meet the Lord," "get filled with the Spirit," "learn the Bible," and to him we pay our tithes and offerings. As Martin Marty observes, "What we tend to have is clienteles instead of congregations."[2]

Under this plan, we hear more and more about being a part of the universal church—that great undefinable, unlocatable body of Christ that mystically exists all over the world. It's a *spiritual* body, we are told. But the thought of it meeting *physically* to worship the Lord, or the idea that it might provide a definite place for service and accountability and even discipline—well, "we just want to be free in the spirit."

French sociologist and political philosopher, Jacques Ellul, speaks to this issue so clearly when he writes:

> Some will try to dissociate the spiritual situation from the material one, despising the material situation, denying that it has any meaning, declaring that it is neutral and does not concern eternal life, and that we can turn our attention solely to "spiritual problems." Such people argue that nothing matters but "the interior life": that is, that to be the "salt" or the "light" is a purely spiritual affirmation, which has no practical consequences. This is exactly what Jesus Christ calls hypocrisy. It means giving up any attempt to live out one's religion in the world. It turns the living person of Jesus Christ into an abstraction. God has become incarnate—it is not for us to undo His work. This dissociation of our life in the two spheres: the one "spiritual", where we can be "perfect", and the other material and unimportant; where we behave like other people, is one of the reasons why the churches have so little influence on the world.[3]

And though I will say more about it later in the book, let me at least introduce the thought here: The problems you may be having in your spiritual life are not caused because your physical body is evil. It is not. Your physical body never has been your enemy, and it never will be. Your problem, my problem, the common enemy of us all, is sin. When sin is allowed to reign in our mortal bodies, [4] of course our bodies will become instruments of unrighteousness. But conversely, when Christ reigns over us, our bodies become His property and once again become instruments of righteousness. Being physical, then, is not our problem. Our downfall has been that sin has gotten into our mortal members.

In His sovereign wisdom our Creator-God has willed that there be a physical side to being spiritual. He has caused us to inhabit flesh. He has made us to live in the midst of His majestic creation. He has commanded us to love Him with all our heart, soul, strength, and mind—and our neighbor as ourselves. He has called us to walk with Him. He has exhorted us to sing psalms and spiritual songs, to bow before Him, to be responsible in business, to visit the widows and the prisoners. Those are more than *just* spiritual exercises. They involve our physical selves as well.

In the pages that follow we will go back to the beginning and see how God in His infinite wisdom established us in the midst of a physical creation as real, live people. We will discuss the Fall and the physical ramifications involved in our straying from Him. We will talk about the many physical means God has used to try and get our attention and bring us back into His kingdom. We will remember that His ultimate method of ransom was the sending of His Son to become physical man: the Lord Jesus Christ, born of a human mother and invading a material world to save real people.

Finally we will discuss the fact that spiritual birth also involves being born into a new nation, a new race, a royal priesthood—God even calls us living stones—people who together form the body of Jesus Christ on this physical planet. We will talk about the entrance into that family, what mealtime there is like, and how to cooperate with the Holy Spirit in carrying out God's will. We will close with a challenge to return to the foundations laid down for us by our fathers in the holy faith.

For nothing happens in the visible and sensible sphere which is not ordered, or permitted, from the inner, invisible, and intelligible court of the most high Emperor, in this vast and illimitable commonwealth of the whole creation.

Augustine of Hippo

2

THE
SPIRITUAL GOD AND
THE PHYSICAL WORLD

Jesus said, "God is spirit; and those who worship Him must worship in spirit and truth."[1] There is no question about it: unless we mortal, physical creatures take on spiritual life through a relationship with Jesus Christ, there is no way for us ever to commune with God. And the Scriptures further teach, "He who has the Son has the life; he who does not have the Son of God does not have the life."[2]

But we must also realize that this God who is spirit made a physical creation in which our communion with Him is to happen. In His creation of mankind, God did not create a class of spirit-beings, personalities without bodies who would navigate in an ethereal cosmos to carry out His will. Rather, He was building a relationship with humanity, and in doing so He made us physical and placed us in a physical creation.

For years scholars and theologians have argued about the mechanics of God's creation and how it took place. Even among those of us who take the biblical account as our basis for truth, there has been diversity of opinion. For example, some hold to a literal "twenty-four-hour day" creation. Others favor a "day-age" theory, in which each of the six days of creation were periods of time instead of literal twenty-four-hour periods. Then there are

those who adhere to the theory of a "pre-Adamic race," in an effort
to explain why geological and anthropological discoveries seem to
date further back than many Christians would care to place creation.

But regardless of how they interpret the biblical account of
God's creation, there is one thing to which virtually all Christians
who take it seriously would agree: God took *nothing* and somehow
made *something* out of it. And we have our magnificent material
world to bear witness to that fact. To quote Anthony Bloom:
"Christianity is the only true materialism, because Christianity is
the only religion which takes matter seriously."[3]

THE MATERIAL AND THE SPIRITUAL

The scriptural account opens with these familiar words: "In
the beginning God created the heavens and the earth. And the
earth was formless and void, and darkness was over the surface of
the deep; and the Spirit of God was moving over the surface of the
waters."[4] God got things started with a formless, nonetheless
material, earth and real water. But things were not *all* material, for
the Holy Spirit was present and moving upon the face of the
waters. It was from the Godhead, then, that the physical and the
spiritual emerged.

And though we confess it is a mystery, all three Persons of the
Godhead were active in creation. The Father was there, for the
Scriptures teach, "For since the creation of the world His invisible
attributes, His eternal power and divine nature, have been clearly
seen, being understood through what has been made, so that they
[the people] are without excuse. For even though they knew God,
they did not honor Him as God, or give thanks; but they became
futile in their speculations, and their foolish heart was darkened."[5]
The Son was there, for Paul says of our Lord Jesus Christ, "For in
Him all things were created, both in the heavens and on earth,
visible and invisible, whether thrones or dominions or rulers or
authorities—all things have been created through Him and for
Him."[6] And the Holy Spirit was present in the creation, for "the
Spirit of God was moving over the surface of the waters."[7]

As the ancient account in Genesis continues, on the second

day the expanse of heaven is separated from the earth; on the third day, the dry land sprouts vegetation and trees and seedbearing plants of all varieties; on the fourth day, the two great lights are made, the sun and the moon; and on the fifth day the waters teem with fish and birds fly over the earth itself—living creatures, "all things bright and beautiful," have been brought into existence.

THE CENTRALITY OF HUMANITY

Now the question comes—at least from our point of view—how do you govern and control all of this? Could not God Himself control it? The answer, of course, is a resounding yes. But He chose to govern His physical creation, called earth, *through* physical means, and we know the identity of that means all too well: *humanity.* The eternal, all-knowing, all-powerful, ever-present, loving, just, and holy God chose to express Himself through human beings, the highest order of physical creation. He could have done it differently, but the fact remains that He did not.

On the sixth day, God said, "Let Us make man in Our image, according to Our likeness; and let them rule over the fish of the sea and over the birds of the sky and over the cattle and over all the earth, and over every creeping thing that creeps on the earth."[8]

God created people, male and female, in His very image. The Founder and Director of the physical earth put specific supervisors in charge of His handiwork. And we are they!

When God surveyed His handiwork and beheld that "it was very good,"[9] humanity was included in His assessment. And though later we were marred by sin, in Christ that divine pronouncement over us is once again in effect. And with this new goodness which we have in Christ, how important it becomes for us to know "It is He who has made us, and not we ourselves."[10] Our goodness in His sight stems from His handiwork and His glorious redemption, not from any merit or correct behavior inherent within us.

But having said this, I must also caution that we must not think of ourselves more *lowly* than we ought! I wonder if the rash of self-help, self-improvement, and self-image courses and instructors on the scene today means we have done just that: come to despise the creation of God which we are. Whereas the Scriptures teach, "No one ever hated his own flesh, but nourishes it and cherishes it, just as Christ also does the church."[11]

How often we have heard it said that Christ hates the sin and loves the sinner. If this is so, who are we to turn around and despise both? Those purveyors of a false humility who, in the name of Jesus, teach people to loathe themselves, to crush their souls, to despise their flesh will come under an awesome scrutiny at the judgment of God. How preposterous to take the creation of God and, under the guise of spirituality, make it a sham—as if it were the work of a demon.

You, everything you are—including your physical body—are precious in the sight of God. Physically, you are a masterpiece of His creative hand. And you had better bring that viewpoint of both God's creation and redemption of yourself into your marriage, or your relationship will quickly begin to suffer and erode. For you are God's personal gift to your mate; as a matter of fact, he or she is given authority over your physical body: "The wife does not have authority over her own body, but the husband does; and likewise also the husband does not have authority over his own body, but the wife does."[12]

If you view your body as second-rate, you are not only calling down God's handiwork, but you are insulting the choice of the person you say you love. Television and magazine ads do not determine human worth, nor are they a worthy measuring stick for physical beauty. That is God's business. He made you just as you are, and you need to thank Him for doing so and be satisfied. If you are married, you are God's choice gift to your husband or your wife. Don't try to be somebody you are not, for that is a denial of God's creative miracle. Instead, be yourself in the power of the Holy Spirit. And enjoy being the present your mate received as a personal gift from a loving Father.

By creation, then, we are a mark of God's glory. In the Eastern church humanity is called "God's icon," while the faithful of the West confess that we are bearers of His image. By redemption, we are brought back on display through the blood of Jesus Christ. And more than being mere showpieces, we are called upon by God to rule and govern on the earth—while at the same time, we who are His people are to submit ourselves to His kingly reign over us.

A CONTINUAL REMINDER

Not only are the things of earth present for people to master, but they are also there as a constant reminder to us that God is there and that His character is reflected in what His hands have made. Thus the physical creation becomes doubly important: it is our supply source of food and clothing, the garden in which we ourselves grow so to speak, and it is that which speaks forth the glory of God even to those who are in apostasy and thanklessness. The creation is always there to remind us of our roots in the mighty God who has made us.

Why did God take such special care that His handiwork would show forth His glory? In Psalm 19 we have the answer; this passage is the *theology* of God's creation—why it looks the way it does. "The heavens are telling of the glory of God; and their expanse is declaring the work of His hands."[13] The "glory of God," His radiance, is visible to His people in and through the things which He has made. These, too, though in a lesser way than humanity, are the bearers of His image.

God's message is one message. The spoken word of the gospel, the written message of the Scripture, the prophetic message of the church, the visual physical message of creation itself, all speak exactly the same thing.

Remember when Paul said concerning the creation of God, "For even though they knew God, they did not honor Him as God, or give thanks; but they became futile in their speculations and their foolish heart was darkened. Professing to be wise, they became fools"?[14] In one sense, the physical creation of God is a crossroads for the human race. For it is when we come face to face with this creation that we choose either (1) to give thanks to the Lord for His glory as exhibited in this remarkable earth or (2) to willfully turn on Him or ignore Him and say this "creation" just happened by itself.

In doing the latter, we end up relating only to the creation, not the Creator, and thus succumbing to idolatry—selfishly enshrining and ultimately ripping off creation instead of responsibly receiving it. It is at this point that foolish hearts become darkened, and God gives the race over to every imaginable kind of atrocity they desire to devise. And this brand of ultimate and near-ultimate sin is very much present in our contemporary culture.

Have you ever heard the objection, often coming from the unbeliever who is trying to get off the hook for not being committed to Christ, "Well, what about all the people on the earth who have never heard?" There are no such people! Because God continually reveals Himself through His creation, nowhere on the earth is the voice of God silent.

This is not to say, as some have suggested, that God is fully knowable through His creation. Nor is this an apologetic for the "I feel close to God Sunday morning on the golf course" boys. Rather, it is to say that the creation of God speaks out His presence and tips us off that we are accountable to Him. And if a person's heart is softened to God as His handiwork is acknowledged in His creation, most likely that same heart will gladly respond to believe the Word of God as it is heard in the gospel of Jesus Christ.

On the other hand, if our hearts already belong to God, the creation serves to make us grateful. I recall a friend from Chicago who, the morning after he committed his life to Christ, stepped outside and realized, "I've never seen the trees before." I find that the older I get, the more I appreciate driving across the countryside and communing with the Lord through the reminder-vehicle of that for which He said we should give thanks: His physical creation.

There is no question that living out in the country, as my family and I have for the past seven years, has helped tremendously my attitude of thankfulness toward the Lord for His earth. Having lived in cities all our lives—first in Minneapolis, and later in Chicago and Memphis—we had sensed the leading of the Lord to move to a small town nestled in the countryside where we could raise our six children and have the opportunity to spend more time together as a family. Country living seemed almost too good to be true.

During the first week in our new habitat, a neighbor came

over to offer us free access to her garden. It was June, and the early crops were already in. I rounded up my three oldest children, and we drove over to her plot, some three blocks away. We spent the next hour or so harvesting spinach, turnips, radishes, cabbages, and a host of other vegetables.

On the way back home, my son Greg, who was at that time eight years old, turned to me and said, "Dad, I thought vegetables came out of cans."

I've never forgotten that. *Of course,* that's what he would think. The only way vegetables ever came into view for him was in a tin can. In the days and weeks and now years that have followed, it has been a special joy for me to take my children fishing, walking in the woods—seeing and hearing and tasting and touching and smelling the handiwork of God in the midst of His marvelous creation.

What a privilege it is to worship the Lord by saying, with a grateful heart, "Thank You for the loveliness of Your handiwork and for caring enough to place me and my family and my fellow-saints in the midst of all this to live out our lives before You." The physical earth is there in part to evoke thanks from us and praise towards God.

Thus, it is no wonder the ancient Tertullian wrote:

> The object of our worship is the one God who created the whole massive structure with all its apparatus of elements, bodies, and spirits: who fashioned it out of nothing through his word, by which he gave the command; through his design, by which he arranged the whole; by his power, by which he could effect his plan, to make it the adornment of his own majesty.[15]

In Psalm 19, David says the sun comes out of its chamber each day with the same glow, showing forth the brightness and the warmth of the Creator. Thus, the physical creation with its imagery and its form shows forth the very glory of the One who made it. In a real sense, the sun and the moon, the stars and the heavenly expanse are all *vestments* which display God's majesty. They are vehicles or means through which His power and glory are expressed. God is Spirit, and He makes Himself known through physical means. And *the fact that the creation is orderly and splen-*

*did and enormously beautiful is vitally important to our under-
standing of what God is like.*

MAINTAINING THE CREATION

Because God willed that spiritual life be carried out in a physical setting, there is one more thing that must be said of the creation: We who are born of God and know Him are specially charged
with taking the best possible care of His handiwork. For we are not
only the rulers, but the custodians as well.

On the political level, this involves keeping effective use from
becoming abuse. It is proper for the people of God to call for
legislation which protects the land from enemies, ranging from
littering on the highways to rape of the land by strip mining which
leaves the landscape with open gouges. On the other hand, an
excessive conservationism which keeps the creation of God from
being effectively used for mankind, or which places more emphasis
upon protecting animals than on insuring the well-being of humanity, can soon approach idolatry. If sloganeer we must, I find no
objection to "Use, Don't Abuse."

In the commercial arena, we can stand above the spirits of
affluence and greed in our day which have often led to a "success at
any cost" mentality. I honestly believe those who pollute the
atmosphere, the land, and the waters of the earth under the banner
of progress and prosperity will be called upon to answer before the
throne of God. As the people of God, let us be exemplary in every
way in the manner in which we conduct our business and utilize
raw materials. In giving us dominion in this sphere, God has not
given carte blanche to buy and sell the earth. Or to mercilessly
obliterate those in competing operations. Or to build kingdoms of
our own. For such behavior bespeaks one who has not brought his
own body and soul under the reign and rule of Christ.

On the personal level, our view of the creation and the Creator determines in large measure how we care for our houses and
property. Again, there are two extremes which face us: the "golden
calf approach," where one has a home and yard designed to upstage
Eden, or the "Beverly Hillbilly syndrome," where the front yard is
a parking lot and the back yard is a dump. How you maintain what

you call yours not only speaks out for your God, but also helps to salt and light those who live nearby.

In Indianapolis, a number of families in an exciting, active church were persuaded by the Holy Spirit to establish their homes in community near the center of town. To date, these people have bought up over thirty old, but sturdy, homes in a depressed inner city neighborhood, and have begun fixing them up. And guess what! The neighbors are tidying up their places, too. In less than a year, the entire neighborhood has shown visible progress in physical improvement. Call it "keeping up with the Joneses"—call it a good kind of leavening. But the way God's people relate to His creation bears a visible influence even upon their earthly neighbors.

As through a conquered man our race went down to death, so through a conqueror we ascend to life.

Irenaeus

3

WHAT
A PATTERN!

To me, the most astonishing thing about God creating human beings is that God made us in His *own* image and likeness. For in all the universe, to whom would you rather bear resemblance than to your Creator and Sustainer? Being patterned after any other creature cannot compare to the glory of being created in the image of the Most High.

However, to say that we possess the image of God only in our physical bodies is inaccurate. For at the point of creation, neither the Father, nor the Son, nor the Holy Spirit was embodied in any sort of physical form as we would know it. The Father, who no person has seen at any time, was described by the ancients as "the fountainhead" of the Trinity. From Him was begotten the eternal Son of God, the Word, who fully shares the divine nature, yet who never, prior to His sojourn on earth, had assumed human flesh as His own. And from the Father eternally proceeds the third person of the Godhead, the blessed Holy Spirit, who was and is without physical form. Thus, we cannot say we have been created in the image of God in the physical sense alone.

But by the same token, it is also a misstatement to say that we bear resemblance to God only in the realm of the soul or the spirit. Instead, God chooses to express Himself through everything that

31

we are—body, soul, and Spirit. Thus, the Scriptures encourage us to yield Him our bodies,[1] our minds,[2] our hearts,[3] our extremities,[4] our tongues,[5] our hearing,[6] and all the rest—for it is the total person which carries His image.

Furthermore, when Scripture says man is in the image of God, it obviously does not mean only males. For God created man both male and female. In fact, if we lose the male-female designation, we forfeit the clarity of His image. But mark well the fact that the God whose image is carried by a male and female humanity is, nonetheless, He.

Those who would like to rewrite the Bible to extract the male designations of Him, His, and He from God will rob Him of His Fatherhood and His headship in the Trinity. In fact, they will end up robbing women of their dignity, because when there is no Father, there is no Mother—to say nothing of the eternal vacuum produced by no Son. For Paul called the heavenly Jerusalem "our mother."[7] John called her "the wife of the Lamb."[8] And even on earth, the church is never he, but always she.

As it is in heaven, so it is to be on earth. Muddy the identity of God in either place and you produce damnable heresy and, as a result, man himself will lose his bearings. If we do not keep our sexual distinctions secure under the Lordship of God's Son, if we follow the rootless philosophies which attempt the blending of male and female, it will end up costing identity loss for all of us—brothers and sisters.

THE PLACE OF HUMANITY

Perhaps the best-known passage of Scripture which defines the creating of humanity on the earth is:

> Then God said, "Let Us make man in Our image, according to Our likeness; and let them rule over the fish of the sea and over the birds of the sky and over the cattle and over all the earth, and over every creeping thing that creeps on the earth."
>
> And God created man in His own image, in the image of God He created him; male and female He created them.
>
> And God blessed them; and God said to them, "Be fruitful and multiply, and fill the earth, and subdue it; and rule over the fish of the sea and over the birds of the sky, and over every living thing that

moves on the earth."

Then God said, "Behold, I have given you every plant yielding seed that is on the surface of all the earth, and every tree which has fruit yielding seed; it shall be food for you;

and to every beast of the earth and to every bird of the sky and to every thing that moves on the earth which has life, I have given every green plant for food"; and it was so.

And God saw all that He had made, and behold, it was very good. And there was evening and there was morning, the sixth day.[9]

As we have established, God set human beings in the midst of a physical creation to reign over it and to show forth the image of God in that surrounding. In fact, as we see later in Genesis, Adam was to name the animal order as well as rule over it.

God created human beings as male and female with the ability to reproduce after their kind. (I sometimes think the only command given by God which man has come close to keeping is, "Be fruitful and multiply." It seems we have no trouble fulfilling this aspect of God's will!) Further, the Lord designed plants to yield seeds and to reproduce and to be the source of food for His new human order and to provide food for the beasts and the birds that moved about the face of the earth.

As we noted earlier, God was very pleased with His physical creation. It came out exactly as He intended it. He meant from all eternity for us to be physical creatures in a physical world.

THE CHARACTER OF GOD

If we, then, are physical people, and yet the physicalness of our nature does not in itself fully represent what we mean by the image of God, just how is His image manifested in us? Exactly what is it that He is after in entrusting such a high calling to us?

Most human illustrations of divine truth have built-in shortcomings. Allowing for this, consider the following: You arise in the morning and look in the mirror. You see yourself reflected there; you see an image of yourself. What you see is not you—that is, the image does not possess skin and bones, hair, life, nor does it have a normal body temperature of 98.6°—it is a *reflection* of you. And just the outer you at that. Your beauty shows up in the mirror as only skin deep. But still we say, "I see myself in the mirror."

And *we* are said to reflect God's image. While that reflection goes beyond the surface to the image of God in our inner person, we do not mean by this that we share in His substance, for we do not. He is uncreated; we are created. He is divine; we are human. We bear His image in that we are alive, we have been given a will, a mind, a set of feelings, all of which go together with all the rest of what we are to say, "This is a living picture of something of what God is like."

On a more personal note, people tell me that my younger son is the "spittin' image of his father." As a matter of fact, he bears my first name. That does not mean, however, that Peter Jon is I. Nor, thankfully, has he been cloned! Instead, he bears resemblance to me. And when we talk about people being made in the image of God, we speak of human persons bearing certain qualities or characteristics of their divine Creator.

In order to understand who we are in relation to God, we must consider God's characteristics, keeping in mind that *though we bear His image, He is forever divine and we are forever human.* As far as the nature of each is concerned, God and humanity are poles apart, for God is the Creator, humanity the creature. God is uncreated with no starting point for existence. Isaiah calls Him "the Everlasting God, the Lord, the creator of the ends of the earth."[10] Humanity is created, and most surely has a beginning. On the other hand, our humanity does carry the image of His divinity. For He says, "You shall be holy, for I the Lord your God am holy."[11]

What, then, are some of the characteristics or qualities of God after which the human race was patterned? Let me choose just a few from what must be a list as infinite as God Himself.

Eternality

Just as God is eternal, so mankind was created to live eternally.

Gregory of Nyssa was a gifted and outstanding thinker in the fourth-century church. He was born in A.D. 330, and in his mid-thirties was appointed bishop of the small town of Nyssa in Asia Minor. Writing to the issue of man bearing God's image of eternality, he said:

Now since one of the good things pertaining to the divine nature is eternity, it was absolutely necessary that the organization of our [human] nature should not be deprived of this attribute, but should contain an immortal element, so that by reason of his innate capacity, man might recognize the transcendent and be seized with a desire for the divine eternity.[12]

In His great priestly prayer, our Lord said, "And this is eternal life, that they may know Thee, the only true God, and Jesus Christ whom Thou hast sent."[13]

You will recall that after the first couple on the earth had sinned, God sent angels to keep man from entering back into the garden and partaking of the Tree of Life.[14] God's concern was that man not live forever in his new state of fallenness, so He protected him with armed cherubim. But now in Christ man dies and lives again, forever. And just like Christ, we will be *physical* forever. As our Lord was raised with a resurrection body capable of eating, bearing nailprints, and being touched, so we at the resurrection of the dead will acquire a new body and will spend eternity bearing the image of God. There is, then, a physical side of living forever!

From the start, God planned for us—indeed, He *created* us—to live eternally. Foreverness was built into us, because the God who created us is eternal. And we shall have bodies with no obsolescence!

Love

Many modern psychologists tell us the two basic needs of human beings are to love and to be loved. This capacity for love was placed by God within our humanity right from the very beginning. We were created to love God, ourselves, and others.

When sin entered, we prostituted the love with which we were created and sought after evil. In fallen humanity, love turned to lust, serving was exchanged for selfishness, and giving for demanding. In the person of our Lord Jesus Christ, the capability for love was restored to the people of God so we could once again be a vivid, living witness that we do bear His image.

And love is far more than an attitude or warm feelings. It is manifested in physical expression as well. Without the physical side of love, as we will see in a later chapter, we cannot adequately reflect the image of God.

Reason

Our God is most assuredly a rational God. In fact, His Son is even called the Reason (Word) of the Father. We who are made in His image were given to reflect this reason that we might know, understand, proclaim, and commune with God. Over sixteen centuries ago, the beloved and devout theologian Athanasius wrote:

> And among these creatures, of all those on the earth, He had special pity for the human race, and . . . He gave an added grace, not simply creating men like all irrational animals on the earth, but making them in His own image and giving them a share in the power of His own Word, so that having as it were the shadows of the Word and being made rational, they might be able to remain in felicity and live the true life in paradise, which is really that of the saints.[15]

Again, this attribute, like the others, was marred by sin. In the Fall, human beings became foolish, losing their ability to reason. This is why Paul was compelled to write to one church in the first century, "For even though they knew God, they did not honor Him as God, or give thanks; but they became futile in their speculations, and their foolish heart was darkened."[16]

It is interesting that in our culture we believe if we can educate people, we will solve the problems of the human race. However this goal has never been achieved, nor will it be. As a matter of fact, it is on the college and university campuses of the world that the seeds of human destruction are most often sown. It was on a college campus that scientists took the atom and its elementary particles, the protons, neutrons, and electrons, and devised the atomic bomb which still threatens to blow us off the face of the earth. Some use of human reason! And it is among the intelligentsia that most of our moral problems are centered. During the sixties the college campus was the seedbed for the drug culture. While today, it is there that sexual exploitation is condoned, taught, and encouraged. What a tragic commentary on higher education.

And yet, through Christ Jesus, our minds can be renewed, and we can reason clearly again. Our thoughts can be guided and controlled by the Holy Spirit. And because we are physical beings, we can carry out our thoughts to benefit the world around us. Thus, we can once again capture that element of His image—godly reason—which has been so tragically lost to us because of sin.

Justice

From the beginning, God has been a just and righteous God. Abraham declared, "Shall not the Judge of all the earth deal justly?"[17] It is comforting to know that God has never made a judicial error. Nor will He. For He is incapable of judging wrongly.

In our humanity, at creation, we possessed the image of God's justice. And, as with the other divine characteristics, there is still a *memory* of this justice residing in the secular culture. We hear the world crying for racial justice, for economic justice, for political justice. But we must realize that the kind of justice which *delivers* men to freedom, which produces true equality, is impossible to attain apart from the presence of the kingdom of God among regenerate people. Even the "limousine liberals" who preach a kind of social justice isolate themselves from the very people they are calling the world to help. Similarly, there are those who hold a biblical view of justice, but who rarely get involved. These are they of whom both Isaiah and Jesus spoke, "This people honors Me with their lips, but their heart is far away from Me."[18]

But let such things never be said of the people of God. What a time in history for the church of Jesus Christ to stand up and not only *preach* justice, but *carry it out* through the lives of its people. For justice has to be physical, not just spiritual; it must be acted out, not just believed. And more and more, Christians appear to be involved in fleshing out the qualities of divine justice which were so paramount in the life of the Lord Jesus Christ. Churches are once again beginning to look after their widows, their poor, their sick. Christian people are embracing brothers and sisters of other races, leaving behind the color barriers of the past.

Holiness

One of the most familiar quotations from both the Old and New Testaments is God's exhortation, "You shall be holy, for I am holy."[19] This is a command, not a platitude. God expects His image-bearers to be like Him in His holiness. What a spectacular possibility for redeemed people! He calls upon us to lay hold of the holiness possible through the work of the Holy Spirit, through our union with Jesus Christ.

Christians, it's time we realized that, while we may not yet be perfected in holiness, we can still by faith do things right. Sin is not inevitable for the Spirit-filled child of God. We are "dead to sin, but alive to God in Christ Jesus."[20] His image in us has been restored, and by the obedience of faith we can show forth His holiness and righteousness in our humanity.

And so it is with all of the qualities of God which He has made available to us. He created us so that these characteristics would be expressed in our humanity; and now by faith in Jesus Christ we may lay hold once again of the godliness which we were created to exhibit. This is why Peter wrote that we are "partakers of the divine nature."[21] While we do not ever share God's divine essence, we nonetheless show forth the riches of His divine grace in our restored humanity.

Does it do anything to you to realize that He has placed these treasures in the earthen vessel known as *you*? Ancient philosophers thought that the human body was the prison-house of the soul. May it never be! That's a *horrid* view of the human frame. House, yes; prison, no. God made our bodies to help express His image. We know this because the eternal Son of God assumed a body just like our own. Our bodies are not shameful and evil vessels unless they are controlled by sin. Rather, they are to be vessels of honor, useful to the Master and prepared for every good work.[22] By the declaration of God, it is a noble thing to be endowed with physical humanity.

TOTAL SIN AND TOTAL GRACE

The closing part of this story we know all too well. Though God created us to reflect His character, His righteousness, the image was marred because of sin. If He had been only just, God would have forever consigned us to darkness. But in His love, He designed a way back to His presence. For the Scriptures say that "where sin increased, grace abounded all the more."[23] When we sin, it is not simply a matter of a spiritual attitude or a mental state, though this is certainly primary. Rather, the whole person sins. Though sin is conceived in the heart, it is brought forth through the body as we give our members over to unrighteousness. When we sin, it is both a physical and a spiritual act. Eve did not ponder the forbidden fruit; she ate it.

Even the tempter, Satan, took the physical form of a serpent. And he made sure he tempted the human race to commit evil acts which involved the physical body, not just the mind. By a physical act—the eating of the forbidden fruit—Adam was lured into disobedience by Satan. It was as though he gave Adam a counter-sacrament as the means of bringing sin to dwell in him.

Thus, the physical side of being spiritual applies to evil as well as to righteousness. Man did not merely *think* sin; he *did* it. And this truth is vital to our understanding of the role of the Lord Jesus Christ in His physical work on our behalf. *For Christ did not merely think righteousness or will righteousness or espouse righteousness in His spirit;* He lived it out for thirty-three years on the face of the earth. And He was crucified in His body on the cross.

It follows, therefore, that when we talk about redemption, we mean physical as well as spiritual redemption. For our bodies as well as our spirits, or our inner selves, need healing from sin's infection. It was through the vehicle of the body that man first disobeyed. It is in the body that he has continued to walk his own way in defiance of God.

The sins of the flesh are numerous: idolatry, fornication, adultery, theft, murder. Such evils need a human body, a physicalness, to bring them to bear. Thinking murder and murdering are two different things (though Jesus Christ condemns both). Thinking fornication and fornicating are not the same. The first involves the mind, the second the body also. Therefore, we are granted a total renovation—body, mind, and spirit—by a Savior who took on Himself all of our humanity.

God made us to be physical as well as spiritual. Therefore, as Paul said, we should glorify God in our bodies.[24] Through Christ our Lord we have greater glory than all the angels, who have remained true to God.

Let's get on with this matter of being redeemed human beings, of being physical people in a physical world who can magnify the Lord in all we say and do.

God, after He spoke long ago to the fathers in the prophets in many portions and in many ways, in these last days has spoken to us in His Son.

The writer of Hebrews

4

BY
ALL MEANS

From Adam to Christ, God used every means conceivable to communicate with the human race. He used people, events, natural phenomena, and miracles. This explains why the writer of Hebrews begins his book, "God, after He spoke long ago to the fathers and the prophets in many portions and in many ways, in these last days has spoken to us in His Son, whom He appointed heir of all things, through whom also He made the world."[1] God spoke "in *many* ways."

The vast majority of the ways in which God has interacted with men in history involve physical phenomena. And as we consider some of these ways, my point is this: *God speaking through physical means is nothing new.* He has done it since time began. In fact, God's normal means of speech on the earth is the physical or material. Furthermore, He continues to speak to us through physical means today.

At this point, let me say something important about miracles in general. In establishing the fact that the spiritual is accomplished in large part through the physical, I want you to notice the cooperation between the Creator and that which is created. To me, the miraculous thing is that God uses the physical to express the spiritual; thus, miracles are both physical and spiritual. In consid-

ering how the physical works in concert under the direction of God
to produce the supernatural, think of Enoch, who walked with God
and was taken miraculously into the Lord's presence.[2] Or, in a
similar vein, Philip who was moved instantaneously from beside
the Ethiopian eunuch over to Azotus where he continued to preach
the gospel.[3] These were two flesh and blood men moved physically
by the power of God.

The miraculous, physical, bodily resurrection of our Lord
Jesus Christ is the first fruit of the resurrection to come. But there
are numerous other instances in which people were brought back
from the dead by the supernatural power of God.[4] Or, think of the
vision which Peter experienced prior to his encounter with Cornelius.[5] Or what about the out-loud voice of God speaking from the
clouds at the baptism of our Lord Jesus, saying, "Thou art My
beloved Son, in Thee I am well-pleased."[6]

So, there are numerous instances where the Spirit of God
worked with man on a very supernatural level. But we must see
that these miracles do not by-pass the physical creation. Instead
they utilize the already existing vehicles which the Lord has made:
stones, donkeys, water, fire, and even locusts!

We have already discussed the important role the physical
creation plays in communicating the love and presence of God to
humanity. The sin of Adam and Eve was manifested in their disobedience to God over the issue of a tree and its fruit, and even
Satan embodied himself in the form of a serpent to deceive earth's
first family. But these events were just the beginning of the em-
ployment of the material to express the spiritual. Let us turn to the
Old Testament and discover how the purposes of God were accomplished in the lives of a sampling of His people.

WOOD AND WATER

When the men of old had gone astray, it would have been easy
for God to come to Noah and say, "I'd like to announce that the
services of the human race are hereby terminated. However, there
are eight of you whom I have chosen to save. I will take you up in
the spirit until I deal with the wicked people. Then I will gently set
you down on earth to begin again." But God did not do this.

Instead, through a dramatic physical miracle, He spared Noah and his family and brought the human race to a wholly new physical start.

To do this, He used rain, water, wood, a dove, an olive branch, and who knows how many animals which He had paired off for the yearlong cruise under Captain Noah's command. The people who perished experienced the spiritual judgment of God physically, while the eight who were preserved experienced the salvation of God in something as physically solid as the ark.[7]

THE PATRIARCHS

Few men in history have experienced the miracles of God as did Abraham, Isaac, Jacob, and Joseph. And yet they, too, experienced the supernatural working of God through natural, physical means.

God had promised Abraham a son who would perpetuate his seed to the extent that his descendants would be more numerous than the stars of the sky.[8] The miraculous element was needed to keep this promise because Abraham's wife, Sarah, was too old to bear children, and Isaac *was* physically born to them. Thus, God used normal, physical means to accomplish His will, though He certainly suspended the physical rules to allow for Isaac's conception.

The day came when God required Isaac, Abraham's long-awaited son.[9] You will remember that the boy and his father had marched up the hill together and, in so many words, the young man said, "Father, you have the sticks and the flint and the wood for the altar, but where is the lamb?"

Abraham gave the reply, "God will provide for Himself the lamb."[10]

And sure enough, a ram caught in the thicket just a few yards away became the sacrifice which God received in substitution for Isaac. That miracle overshadowed the normal, and a material sacrifice was made by an obedient man to the living God: the physical to the spiritual.

Note here, by the way, that even the commands of God are not necessarily static once they are given. He continues to be *actively* Lord of His word, and thus retains the prerogative to issue further commands in midstream. What an example we have here of the difference between living by rigid legalism and living under the active reign of a living God who speaks. Had Abraham been a legalist, he would have gone ahead and killed his son as a sacrifice—and then thanked God for providing the ram as well!

THE WRESTLER

An interesting combination of the corporeal and the non-corporeal comes in the wrestling match which took place between Jacob and the angel. That angel may well have been a spiritual being without a body, though it would not appear so from the text. But one thing is crystal clear: the *struggle* was not just spiritual; it was physical as well! To say otherwise would leave one hard-pressed to explain Jacob's disjointed hip.

So often we see our struggles *only* as spiritual or mental. We say, "I struggled with that in my mind for several days." Or, "This situation has certainly troubled my spirit." I'm not denying that there can be struggles that are fundamentally internal. But I'm wondering if we have so many *internal* struggles because we ignore or flee from *external* struggles. We seem frightened of the physical.

Take, for example, the whole issue of confrontation. The Scriptures teach that when we have aught against our brother, we go to him and make it known. Then, if a proper response is not given, we're told to take someone else along. Ultimately the issue is to be brought before the whole church if it can't be resolved privately.[11]

I don't believe for a moment that this is a pat formula to be used every time there's a problem between two people. Certainly there is the latitude of the Spirit's guidance in all of this. But most of us Christians (and I am certainly including myself) have been afraid of nose-to-nose, toes-to-toes confrontation. We'd rather "pray about" a problem than deal with it.

Jacob certainly didn't cower and passively allow God's angel to take him down for the count! As a matter of fact, Jacob *won!* Similarly, Nathan the prophet didn't hide what he knew God had given him to say. He confronted King David with his guilt of murder, lying, and adultery by saying to his face, "You are the man!"[12] Centuries later, Paul did not hide his convictions when he suspected Peter was slipping back into legalism; Paul told the Galatians, "I opposed him to his face. . . ."[13]

It's high time that we believers learn to wrestle again. Having become so "spiritual" in our modern development, it's time we learn to get more totally involved.

I am reminded of a report which came to me from a church in one of our southern cities. Several years ago, after many attempts to restore a young man to spiritual health, the elders were forced to expel him from the church for repeated sexual misconduct. (Of course, as is usually the case with the unrepentant, he told many people of the "harsh, ungracious treatment" he had received. I mention this for the sake of those who have taken godly discipline seriously and have been maligned. The howl of the wounded canine is highly predictable!)

Two or three years went by and little was heard either from the man or about him. Then one day word came that he was engaged to marry a girl in another city, a girl who was known for her love for Christ. When the leaders of the church from which he had been excommunicated heard the report, they contacted the government of the other church involved, namely the pastor who was to perform the wedding ceremony.

A letter was drafted to the minister, explaining the discipline that had been administered years earlier to the man, asking that it be honored. "If the man has turned from his sin and come back to Jesus Christ, then we would want to know this from him that the matter might be cleared," the letter said.

The pastor checked first with the prospective bridegroom and then with his friends. It turned out that not only had he gone from bed to bed since his removal from the first church, but he was having sex with another woman during his engagement to the Christian girl. The wedding was called off, the young woman was spared sure heartache for the future, and the people of God gave thanks for the Lord's intervention.

What impressed me in this whole series of events was the

pattern of a lack of aggressive, physical, concrete action in *my* life as a Christian in dealing with such matters. It has always been so much easier not to get involved because of the trouble it could cause. Or I'd use prayer as a cop-out and say, "I'll ask God to work it out." I have been way too passive, and I suspect that's true with most of us. It is far easier to be "spiritual" and not allow ourselves to come into contact with touchy situations. But such a stance is worse than useless.

THE PROTO-HISTORIC CHARLETON HESTON

How can you get more physical in your spirituality than Moses? It seems that every time he turned around, God used one more physical phenomenon to accomplish His will in the lives of the children of Israel.

The instances are almost too numerous to mention: (1) the burning bush; (2) the parting of the Red Sea; (3) the cloud and the pillar of fire; (4) the finger of God writing the Decalogue upon tablets of stone. To quote Shakespeare, "What, will the line stretch out to the crack of doom?"

If ever we were given living proof that God uses physical means to accomplish His will, it would be during those years our forerunners spent in the wilderness. I suppose my favorite story in the whole, unfolding drama is the incident of the elders and the quail in Numbers 11. If you want some interesting bedtime reading, get a modern paraphrase, such as the Living Bible or the Good News Bible, and go through this incredible chapter. Without going into great exegetical detail, two lessons come across vividly.

First of all, God uses human leadership to establish spiritual authority among His people. Moses was about ready to give up because the responsibilities for what may well have been two million Israelites were too great. (The Numbers 11 text records 600,000, but this count was of military personnel only.) God's solution to the whole problem came after Moses had simply asked the Lord to be merciful and end his responsibility by taking his life. Instead, God told Moses to select from the elders seventy men who could stand with him in the leadership of the nation.

I get so tired of people saying, "I don't need any human authority to tell me what to do. All I need is the Holy Spirit." Where on earth do they get such an idea? Not from the Holy Bible! What arrogance and ignorance! Just a cursory reading of the Scriptures makes it clear that God's authority is expressed through godly people—real, live, flesh-and-blood people. That has *always* been the way God's guidance comes to His congregation on the earth, whether in the Old Covenant or in the New. It was true in Israel, it was true in the early church, and it is still true today.

I'll tell you, the more I grow spiritually, the more I want to be under godly authority. Those who are looking for a leaderless, headless Christianity, where everyone does his own thing, had best remember the promise of our Lord that when He returns to the earth, He will rule with an iron rod.[14] *That's* authority!

Those who are members of the family of God, who welcome His coming and His reign, are promised that the government of God for all eternity will be ruled by a triumvirate. Therefore, it stands to reason that it is well for us to learn to live under authority now. Such is found in the holy church of Jesus Christ.

The second lesson we learn in Numbers 11 is that God has a sense of humor. At least it seems that way to me 3500 years later. The people were tired of manna; they murmured and complained. They had baked it, breaded it, broiled it, and steamed it. They couldn't even stand to look at it anymore, let alone eat it. All they could think of were the salads, fruits, and meat they had left in Egypt. They wanted meat!

And I want to tell you, God answered them physically! He sent quail. Boy, did He send quail. Scholars argue over whether the quail in Numbers 11 were three-feet-deep on the ground or whether they flew in three feet off the ground. Regardless, God sent so many quail their way that it took the people two days and a night to pick up thousands of the birds. The people ate quail until it was coming out their ears.

It all began when the greedy people asked for meat, and their request was granted. Then Moses asked to be relieved from duty. Instead, he got additional personnel. God answered both requests exceeding abundantly, above all that they could ask or think! And in both cases, be it for reward or for punishment by death, God answered physically as well as spiritually.

THE WORLD'S FIRST URBAN DEVELOPMENT PLAN

In the Book of Numbers we have the greatest outdoor camping program in all of history. For those of you who have served in the armed forces, can you imagine a bivouac for forty years?

Despite their disobedience and hardness of heart, God did not forsake the Israelites—those rebellious souls who tramped the wilderness for forty years.

In fact, to better govern His people, God instructed that they be divided up by tribes and units. All two million of them. Groupings of people were given specific tasks to carry out.[15] When each day was over, there was no question in the minds of the people as to which tent they were to return to. Everything was carefully blocked off: three tribes in the north, three in the south, three in the east, and three in the west.

There are those in the church today who are saying, "Let's not be organized. Let's just flow in the Spirit." The Scriptures have an expression for that: "Every man doing whatever is right in his own eyes."[16] This was not to be the case in Israel, nor is it to be the case in the church today.

God's solution then was to group the Hebrews by tribes and by units of thousands, hundreds, fifties, and tens. Thus, each person knew where he belonged and how he fit. There was a definite organization of the children of Israel. Their cohesiveness and effectiveness as a spiritual nation was vitally linked to their physical organization. Amazingly, when you read through the Book of Judges, you will find that when their physical order was at an all-time low, their spiritual impact responded with a commensurate ineptness.

You say, "Well, then, what's the answer? If God's will is opposed to both the 'make things happen' and the 'let things happen' philosophies, what's the solution?" God's purpose in this age is for His people to operate under the lordship of Jesus Christ, and that involves the authority He establishes in His church: bishops, district superintendents, pastors, deacons, stewards—whatever you may call them.

There is certainly nothing wrong with spontaneity; nor is there anything wrong with human freedom, for God has given us an abundance of both. But freedom and spontaneity are to operate *within* certain boundaries.

We moderns say, "Don't fence me in!" The assumption is that church order eliminates spontaneity. However, a fence actually promotes spontaneity because it gives us a *safe, definitive area* within which to be spontaneous.

Jesus used the metaphor of sheep and shepherds. In John 10, the sheep which He was talking about were kept by shepherds who guarded the sheepfold. This was to protect them from the wolves and to give them a safe area in which to graze. You see, inside the fence were peace and security; outside were ravines and ravenous beasts. And so it is in the church. God's order always provides the boundary inside which we can experience His green pastures and His still waters. And the shepherds are there to protect us as we go about our daily lives.

Can you imagine a self-asserting sheep in the flock saying, "It just isn't right for me to be fenced in like this. I need to be free, out there where I can truly express myself. I'll just wander out here . . . um . . . as the Spirit moves and be fulfilled." The only thing that will be fulfilled is the wolf's appetite—as evidenced by a lot of the people of God today who are trying to be spiritual outside of the historic church with its physical care and protection, its physical leadership.

A THRONE FOREVER

We cannot forget King David. God found in David a man whose heart was so true that He told him He would establish his throne forever—a throne to which the Lord Jesus Christ Himself would become the ruling heir. David was a member of the lineage out of which our Messiah was to come.

Prior to ascending to the monarchy, David learned well his lessons in trusting and obeying God. Any of us who have ever darkened the door of a Sunday school class know the story of the young shepherd boy killing Goliath.[17] Though it was a physical killing, using a real stone and a real slingshot, when the tale is told today the following theme usually emerges: "Be faithful to God in the little things, and then when the giants come along—the big tests—you'll find it far easier to obey Him."

The point is well-taken; the lesson is utterly true. But the lesson involves more than a heart attitude to resist evil. For when push comes to shove, unless our heart attitudes manifest themselves in real, live victories out there in the everyday world, we could fall into the trap of being hearers of the Word only and not doers.

When I speak of resisting evil, I have in mind the many enemies who stand against humanity in general and the people of God in particular. I think, for example, of false prophets in the past, such as Mary Baker Eddy, Charles T. Russell, and Joseph Smith; and in the present, Sun Myung Moon, Witness Lee, and Victor Paul Wierwille, founder of The Way International.

This brings us face-to-face not just with factual error but with personalities as well. If contending for the Christian faith were only a matter of one ideology against another, things would be far more comfortable. But Satan implants what Paul calls "doctrines of demons"[18] inside of real, live people. There are both false prophecies and false prophets.

Frankly, it goes back to that matter of confrontation. Except that now we're not talking about brother to brother or sister to sister confrontation, but about warfare between the people of God and those within the kingdom of darkness.

It is no fun at all to withstand an enemy face-to-face. But sometimes it must be done. And Christ promises: "But when they deliver you up, do not become anxious about how or what you will speak; for it shall be given you in that hour what you are to speak. For it is not you who speak, but it is the Spirit of your Father who speaks in you."[19] You'll find that the more faithful you are in standing for Him against the privates in Satan's army, the better you'll fare if called upon at a later date to confront the colonels and the generals. For the doctrinal Goliaths are legion!

THE RULERS AND THE PROPHETS

Israel's history continues on with many amazing events occurring in the lives of its rulers and its prophets. In 931 B.C. the one nation became two as it was divided into the northern kingdom, (Israel), ultimately to come under the control of the Assyrian government, and the southern kingdom (Judah), which was to undergo seventy years of Babylonian captivity starting in 586 B.C.

It was in the years just before, during, and just after the Babylonian captivity that those we call the "minor prophets" conducted their various campaigns on behalf of the kingdom of God. And such mighty warriors they were! Jonah was swallowed by a huge fish; Hosea bought back an adulterous wife out of prostitution and slavery; Jeremiah wept real tears over sin; and Daniel was thrown to wild beasts. As the writer of Hebrews summed it up, these were people "of whom the world was not worthy."[20]

Then came two of the greatest activists God's people have ever known, Ezra and Nehemiah. Again, they, by physical means, carried out the heavenly will of God. It was Ezra who restored and rebuilt the temple during the time of Esther. It was Nehemiah who oversaw the reconstruction of the walls of Jerusalem, a miraculous feat that was carried on against great odds.

All of these are *our* people! They are our ancestors in the family of God. Through the superintending of the Father, Son, and Holy Spirit, they carried on the will of God, pressing it out in the most physical and material of ways. These were not people who sat idly by thinking great thoughts, trying to stir up warm, inspiring feelings. They went far beyond the meditative into the combat zone of kingdom against kingdom.

And so it is with us today: There will be those times when we will hear, "Be still, and know that I am God,"[21] or when Jesus Christ again speaks to His followers and says, "Come away by yourselves to a lonely place and rest a while."[22] But even these are times of physical rest, times of preparation, times of regrouping, not the pattern for a life style designed to reflect a new brand of make-believe.

As real people in a real world, we are being called upon in this day, as our forebears were in ages past, to be the ambassadors of

Jesus Christ in a physical world. And should times of great testing and trial come again upon the church, may we be ready to stand as His servants and soldiers and carry out His spiritual orders in a physical way—perhaps even to suffer and die for Him.

And how has it happened to me, that the mother of my Lord should come to me?

Elizabeth

5

MARY
(OR, PARDON ME WHILE I VENERATE THE MOTHER OF GOD!)

It was now time in Israel's history, "the fulness of time"[1] as the apostle Paul termed it, for God to visit His people in the flesh.

The coming of the Messiah had been foretold for fifteen hundred years prior to the event of His birth. The ancient prophets had spoken of His coming on hundreds of occasions as recorded in the Scriptures, and they had done so with exacting precision.

God's chosen people needed to be rescued from their sins. In His plan, one fully human, yet sinless, was needed—one who could suffer and die as a substitute for all mankind. And this deliverer must be from the lineage of David to fulfill the prophecy that David's throne would be established forever. But all men on the earth were disqualified because of their own sin; no such mediator could be found in the human race.

Since man was totally incapable of initiating his own deliverance from eternal death or his own reconciliation to God, only God Himself could supply the connection to provide communion between Himself and the human race. Thus, before the earth was even created, God had planned to send His only Son to assume human flesh, to be that man, that Savior. To meet our need and to satisfy His own justice, *God had to become a man.* And since only God can save, the mediator also had to be fully divine.

THE NECESSARY HUMAN VEHICLE

There have been times in history when God has not used humanity as a physical vehicle through which to do His work. For example, a burning bush served the purpose for Moses, a donkey for Balaam. And when the pompous religious bigots of Jesus' day objected to the exuberant hosannas from His disciples at His triumphal entry into Jerusalem, He reminded the complainers that the very stones would cry out if those men were silent.

But this time, with respect to the coming of the Messiah, God chose a human being, a woman, as the means through which His Son might become a man. For unless He had a human mother, the fully divine Son of God could not be a fully human member of our desperate race. And there was another factor involved. Long before, the promise had been made that Messiah would rise up from among God's people, Israel. For God to choose a human mother from another race would be a total denial of the role of God's chosen people in redemption. So God by His own will and promise, chose a woman from the Jewish race.

In modern industry and education, when a new executive officer or college president is to be selected, a search committee is organized. This committee wades through lists of candidates, and after careful scrutiny, a final choice is made.

Somehow, somewhere in the economy of God, the council of the Holy Trinity selected a young woman named Mary to be the God-bearer. As a result, she became the flagship of womanhood for all of history. Then God sent an angel, Gabriel, to inform her that she had been selected as mother of the Son of God. Luke records how it took place:

> The angel Gabriel was sent from God to a city in Galilee, called Nazareth, to a virgin engaged to a man whose name was Joseph, of the descendants of David; and the virgin's name was Mary.[2]

God gave Gabriel specific directions as to where to go to find the mother of our Lord—the city of Nazareth in the province of Galilee. And Mary, a virgin, was already engaged to a man named Joseph, who was a descendant of King David.

This was to fulfill Isaiah's prophecy: "Therefore the Lord Himself will give you a sign: Behold, a virgin will be with child and bear a son, and she will call His name Immanuel." And Jeremiah's prophecy: "I will make a righteous Branch sprout from David's line."[3]

THE VIRGIN BIRTH: NOT AN OPTIONAL TRUTH

Some modern scholars will go the second mile to discredit the virgin birth of Christ. In doing so, they often point to this passage, Isaiah 7:14, and say that the Hebrew word for *virgin* can also be translated *young woman*. But while the Hebrew word can at times be translated *young woman*, such a translation makes no sense in this context.

First of all, Isaiah's prophecy is preceded by the words, "The Lord Himself will give you a sign." What sort of sign is it when a young woman conceives a child? That's no miracle at all!

Secondly, in those days young, unmarried women *were* virgins. In our era, we tend to forget there was a period in human history when the kind of behavior allowed by our promiscuous society would have turned such offenders into a rock pile.

Thirdly, the seventy or more translators of the Septuagint, a translation of the Hebrew Old Testament and Apocrypha into Greek done sometime in the third century B.C., rendered the Hebrew noun *virgin*, not *young woman*.

Finally, Luke says Mary was a virgin, using the Greek word which meant *virgin*.

GABRIEL SAID IT RIGHT!

The angel Gabriel announced to Mary, "'Hail, favored one! The Lord is with you.' But she was greatly troubled at this statement, and kept pondering what kind of salutation this might be."[4] (Those who deny Mary her proper honor are in good company at this point. She, too, stumbled over the angel's greeting!) But she was soon to see why he made such a proclamation.

Today some Christians have trouble echoing the spirit of Gabriel's greeting. But if an envoy from God the Father would give Mary such honor, why should we shrink back? Certainly we do not have higher standards than He! The angel did not worship her; nor are we to worship her. But we are to honor her, call her (as the Scriptures do) blessed, and revere or respect her as the woman God favored to bear His Son. In a word, we *venerate* her. For the angel gave her a most royal salutation and pronounced upon her a lovely blessing. And then he said:

> Do not be afraid, Mary; for you have found favor with God. And behold, you will conceive in your womb, and bear a son and you shall name Him Jesus. He will be great, and will be called the Son of the Most High; and the Lord God will give Him the throne of His father David; and He will reign over the house of Jacob forever; and His kingdom shall have no end.[5]

Gabriel assured Mary she had found favor in the sight of God. This would indicate that our behavior—how we conduct ourselves in these physical bodies in which we live—is noticed by the Lord. While we know we are justified by faith, it is important that we also realize that our life style has great significance in the sight of God.

For example, the Scriptures tell us that Cornelius was attended to by God because of his devoutness and almsgiving.[6] Even though Cornelius still needed Peter to preach the gospel of grace to him, Luke's account shows that it was because of Cornelius's responsible behavior that God singled him out to be hearer and believer of that word—and the first Gentile to be converted. Thus, faith and works must not be seen as separate or isolated categories, for "faith without works is useless."[7]

Mary found great favor in the sight of God because of her holiness *and* physical purity. We cannot get around that point in Scripture: *God honors people for behaving.*

Interestingly, the basic question Mary had was not whether the baby she would bear would be the Son of the Most High God, but rather, how could this miracle happen. She asked Gabriel, "'How can this be, since I am a virgin?' And the angel answered and said to her, 'The Holy Spirit will come upon you, and the power of the Most High will overshadow you; and for that reason the holy offspring shall be called the Son of God.'"[8] Then the angel told her about her relative Elizabeth. By now Elizabeth was in her sixth month of pregnancy, yet she was beyond the years of childbearing—as had been Sarah of old. And Gabriel's comment on the whole matter was, "'For nothing will be impossible with God.'"⁹

As He had done over and over in history, God again chose a human being as the vehicle to carry out His will. And I believe that because Mary had learned to be faithful in the little things, she was now chosen to be faithful and obedient to the highest honor ever bestowed upon a woman. For when she heard the glorious announcement, she said, "Behold, the bondslave of the Lord; be it done to me according to your word."¹⁰ Mary gained even more favor in the sight of God by being submissive to His will.

WHAT SHALL WE CALL HER?

Those of us in the Protestant tradition are now faced with an incredibly important question: Is it proper to call Mary "the mother of God"? The answer hinges on our response to a second question: Who was conceived in her womb? All who know Him would agree it was our Lord Jesus Christ, "the Son of the Most High God."¹¹ For if the baby in her womb was not the eternal Son of the Father, fully God and fully man, we are still in our sins and are bound for an everlasting hell. To confess anything less is to follow another Christ and another gospel. And if we believe that Jesus Christ is God in the flesh, we understand the ancients of our church when they said Mary was the mother of God; *for it was God who was in her womb,* the Second Person of the Godhead, the Word who had been made flesh.

At this point, I need to make two things very clear: (1) To call Mary the mother of God does not mean we are distinctly Roman Catholic in our doctrine. Rather, it is to be *catholic* (that which is believed by Christians everywhere) in our doctrine. (2) To call Mary the mother of God does not mean that she was the originator of the Godhead or of the Second Person of the Godhead. But it most assuredly says that when God the Son was conceived in her womb by the Holy Spirit, He assumed from Mary His flesh—that is, His human nature. And since that baby was very God and very man in one Person, and since Mary is the woman who bore and nourished Him, she most properly wears the title "mother of God."

The most critical ancient challenge concerning Mary's title was brought by an early heretic named Nestorius. He opposed her title "God-bearer" (Greek: *Theotokos*) and wanted her called only the mother of Christ because he held that she was the mother only of Christ's humanity and not of His divinity. The problem with this view is that it splits Jesus up into two persons, the one God and the other man. For this heresy, Nestorius was condemned. Jesus Christ is one Person with two natures: one divine and the other human.

Timothy Ware, an Orthodox theologian, addresses the problem well:

> What Mary bore was not a man loosely united to God, but a single and undivided person, who is God and man at once. The name *Theotokos* (God-bearer) safeguards the unity of Christ's person: To deny her this title is to separate the Incarnate Christ into two, breaking down the bridge between God and man and erecting within Christ's person a middle wall of partition.[12]

However, the ancient church fathers were not the first to recognize Mary as the God-bearer. The initial response of Elizabeth upon receiving Mary in her home and knowing of the imminent birth of the Messiah was, "Blessed among women are you, and blessed is the fruit of your womb! And how has it happened to me, that the *mother of the Lord* should come to see me?"[13]

Nor was it only later in church history that veneration or honor came to Mary, for it was Gabriel, the angel sent from God, who said, "Hail, favored one."[14] Listen once again to Timothy Ware:

> Note that we have termed her "most exalted *among God's creatures*": Orthodox, like Roman Catholics, venerate or *honour* the Mother of God, but in no sense do the members of either Church regard her as a fourth person of the Trinity, nor do they assign to her the *worship* due to God alone [italics his].[15]

It was the doctrines of the immaculate conception of Mary (that she was conceived without sin) and the assumption of Mary (that she was taken to heaven without physical death), however, that became dogmas so very much later—the former in the nineteenth century, the latter in the twentieth century in the

Roman Catholic church. Neither were taught as part of the ancient biblical faith.

MARY—A ROLE MODEL

In the last fifty years, many have willfully embraced the heresy that denies the virgin birth of our Savior. Has this more easily crept in because modern Protestants have failed to give proper honor to Mary? Personally, I believe God has permitted that error to inflict the Protestant camp as judgment against us for robbing Mary of the honor bestowed upon her by God Himself! And there are several things at stake in our treatment of Mary.

First of all, the *truth* is at stake. A proper view of the Person of Christ demands a proper understanding that He is the Incarnate Son of God. And to hold a biblical view of the Incarnation means we must adhere to the truth concerning the role of Mary, His mother. Otherwise, we *separate* the physical from the spiritual.

Salvation is a spiritual matter, but it has its absolutely indispensable physical side. God did not provide redemption for man apart from a human man who was born of a human mother. Take away the physical aspects of salvation, and *you have no salvation.* In fact, it was not even proper to ask which is more important, the physical or the spiritual. They are inseparable parts of God's total provision for our restoration to Him.

Secondly, Mary is a *model for womanhood.* She is the highest example there is of godly womanhood. And Scripture testifies that she is to receive commensurate honor throughout all generations.

Models are incredibly important for personal development. In our family, our oldest daughter sets the pace for our other three girls; our oldest son is the model for our younger son. And, by the grace of God, they are good models. If you have children, you know exactly what I mean. If you are not a parent, just think back to your own childhood; remember how things were? Even if there was not an older brother or sister, there was usually a "bigger kid" in the neighborhood after whom you patterned your life.

The super-saint may say, "Oh, but I don't need a model. I just do what the Holy Spirit tells me."

My answer is, "You mean the Holy Spirit has ceased to use

people in your life?" No, the role model for human beings is other human beings. (Even a bad model can be helpful, as we see the result of sin.) The Lord Jesus Christ in His humanity is the model of righteousness for all humanity in general; for a showcase of womanhood, men and women alike turn to the woman God honored, the blessed Mary.

And let's be practical for a moment. You didn't get to where you are today as a Christian apart from human vehicles. *Of course* the Holy Spirit has been at work in your life. But more often than not, He works through people He has chosen to use. To say otherwise is to say, in effect, "I report only to God. I do not need or heed His people."

Certainly the Lord created us as people He could use to minister to one another, to forward His kingdom. Had He chosen to, He could work *only* in direct fashion; he could serve each of us personally without human helpers. No brothers and sisters. No fathers and mothers in the faith. No Scriptures. No church. No other child of God to care for you, hold you, hurt with you, cry with you, build you up. He *could* have worked a great miracle and done it all by Himself.

But He didn't.

Without Him we can do nothing. And without us, He has chosen in His sovereignty to do very little.

Mary's obedience to the Lord continued throughout her entire life. In fact, she made one of the best statements concerning obedience to Jesus Christ that has ever been made. When they ran out of wine at the wedding in Cana, Mary referred the servants to Jesus and told them, "Whatever He says to you, do it".[16]

If ever womanhood needed some tangible standard by which to navigate through the culture, it most certainly is now. In Mary, a very physical model of a marvelously spiritual godliness is available; she is an example of one woman who was a bond-servant to the Most High God, and who through her obedience and faith has been crowned with honor beyond any woman who has ever lived.

Third, Mary is a *model for teen-agers*. And if ever teen-agers needed a model, it most certainly is today!

In our cultural setting, the junior high and high school years of a person's life are the most difficult. The whole issue of the identity crisis arises as young adults are asking themselves who they are, why they are on the earth, and what their lives should be about. Most young people I meet and counsel with are of the opinion that God doesn't have much use or role for them until they become adults.

In the turbulent years of the sixties, teen-agers rebelled and cried, "Never trust anyone over thirty." Later, someone came up with the slogan, "Never trust a person over *thirteen*." They had turned on parents, on society, and their identity problems increased; soon they discovered they could not trust even themselves. The drop-outs stole one another's clothing, money, and morals. Their sacrament was drugs.

But there is good news: God does use teen-agers. Mary was most likely a teen-ager when she bore the Son of God. Most biblical scholars believe she was about sixteen years of age when she conceived the Lord Jesus, seventeen when she gave birth to Him. And remember Gabriel's tribute to her—she had walked faithfully and obediently with God during the preceding teen-age years.

LET'S GET REACQUAINTED

Someone might well say, "But why is Mary so important?" Or, "How does knowing she is the mother of God relate to my daily Christian life?"

The basic purpose here is not the exaltation of Mary, but rather Mary's baby. To exalt Jesus Christ, however, does not stop with confessing Him as Lord. It also has to do with holding a proper view of who He is. To call Him Lord and see Him as only human will not do. That is no salvation. Nor is He only God and not really human. Nor is He God and a superhuman. No, He is fully God and fully man in one Person.

Losing sight of Mary as the bearer of the eternal Son in His flesh not only strips away her identity, but worse, it muddies the identity of Jesus Christ. For unless it was God and man in one Person who died on the cross for you, you are still in your sins! Establishing the woman Mary as the mother of God firms up the full humanity of Christ. And knowing she was a virgin secures the fact that as the almighty God overshadowed her, the Holy Spirit supernaturally planted within her womb the seed of the flesh which the Son of God assumed as His own. Thus, the Word became flesh and dwelt among us.

To call Mary anything less than the mother of God throws open to question who Jesus Christ is. Thus, knowing who *she* is helps secure who *He* is! And what could be more important to your life and faith than *knowing* Him who is true God and true man?

Having said all this, let me offer four concrete suggestions as to how we who love Christ Jesus can begin to honor His mother.

Pastors: Build a consciousness of Mary among your people through the public reading of the Scriptures concerning her and through your sermons. Encourage people to express their thanks to God for her when they pray—much the same as they have thanked Him for dear loved ones, for those who have influenced their lives for Christ, for what Isaiah or Nehemiah wrote or did, for Paul, and so on. If we can pray, "Lord, thank You for Mrs. Smith and the way she helped me last week," can we not also give thanks to our Lord for His mother who bore Him for our salvation!

Parents: When you teach your children concerning the heroes of the faith in days gone by, tell them of Mary and her obedience to the Lord. Because she has been ignored, take special care to build her up and bring her back to her rightful place in your children's understanding.

Students: Read what the Reformers—men like Luther, Calvin, and Chemnitz—or those who came later—like the Wesleys—had to say about her. See if they did not confess the ancient faith concerning her. Read what those who directly followed the Twelve, the Church Fathers, wrote. And do a study of the inspired Holy Scriptures and read what is said of her, especially in the Gospels.

Doubters: Repent.

I say this sincerely. You have no idea how difficult it was for me to say "uncle" to my previous opinion and come back to the biblical faith of the church on this issue. I have maligned her blessed name, I have poked fun at those who have defended her, and I have been disrespectful to artists' renderings of her. For all of this, I am honestly sorry, I have apologized to God, and hereby go on public record as a man who honors the mother of my Lord.

How good it is to be Mary's friend and fellow-pilgrim once again!

He did not cease to be God by being born as man, or fail to be man by remaining God.

Hilary of Poitiers

6

OUR
PHYSICAL GOD

Face it: God is after holiness in our lives. Though at the beginning of His work in our lives He forgives us of all our sins—past, present, and future—His work with us certainly is not finished at that point. For He seeks to take these purified vessels and make them, as the Scripture says, "sanctified, useful to the Master, prepared for every good work."[1] In short, He wants us righteous in both our standing with Him and in the lives that we live.

We have tended to stop with the former. We have often preached only an imputed or declared righteousness which assures us that we are acceptable in the sight of God—a doctrine which is gloriously true—and have stopped there. But because that doctrine is true, we have the "spiritual equipment" to see righteousness concretely expressed—that is, through good deeds, a clean heart, the fruit of the Spirit—in our daily living. Or, to put it another way, upon the foundation of being *declared* righteous, we can build a visible life style of *living out* righteousness. And it is no secret that we who call ourselves evangelical, born-again, committed Christians have fallen miserably short in this respect.

Let me be specific.

The way we Christians behave in our marriages is scandalous. Divorce among evangelical Christians is reaching epidemic proportions. The other evening as several close friends and I were discussing this, we counted up twenty-four well-known evangelical *leaders* who have been divorced in the past two years. As the shepherds go, so go the sheep.

And not only is divorce rampant, but by and large the church has been silent when it comes to doing anything about it. We have lost holiness and righteousness in our view of the sanctity of Christian marriage. How often have we accepted this line of rationalization as a legitimate excuse: "My needs are not being met." Since when has the object of marriage been "getting your needs met"?

We have been tamed by our culture. We have not been righteous, but have stood by while evangelical marriage after evangelical marriage goes down the drain.

Or what about the way we look after our bodies? It is incredible to me that a person with a fat, overstuffed body can stand up and talk about "coming under the lordship of Jesus Christ"; this person's body has no more been brought under the reign of Christ than has the body of the drunk slumping on a stool at the corner bar. Today's crop of believers are not, as a people, known as those who have their bodies under control. We are little, if any, better than the world in this area.

Furthermore, we are not looking after the physical and spiritual needs of our poor. The tendency in the contemporary Christian church has been that when someone speaks out for the destitute or unemployed (and I don't mean those who are willfully lazy), someone else drops the accusation that he is lapsing back into the "social gospel." Well, then, let's call it the *physical gospel*. It was our Lord, after all, who not only said He came to preach the gospel to the poor, but made sure they were cared for while He was on the earth—and continued that ministry as head of the church after His ascension. That's what the widows-and-orphans passages in the New Testament are all about.

THE PLAN FOR HOLINESS

If a person is truly born of the Spirit, he inwardly desires to be holy. And all of us have experienced the great personal disappointment when we are not. Has God made provision for us to bring our bodies and minds under His control that we might experience the joy of living righteously? Can we really *be* holy? Can we learn to say "no" to sin and "yes" to Christ? The answer is an unqualified, emphatic *yes!*

If the answer to that question were not a powerful yes, the Scriptures would not tell us to put aside "all malice and all guile and hypocrisy and envy and all slander."[2] Nor would they teach us to "bridle the whole body."[3] Nor would we read, "Do you not know that your bodies are members of Christ?"[4] You see, these are all physical manifestations of being holy.

So what's the secret? How does God give us this holiness? Ironically, it is the apostle who may have wavered the most during his three-year earthly walk with Jesus Christ who gives us the answer! We are told by Peter that God, in His divine power,

> has granted to us everything pertaining to life and godliness, through the true knowledge of Him who called us by His own glory and excellence. For by these [His glory and excellence] He has granted to us His precious and magnificent promises, in order that by them you might become partakers of the divine nature, having escaped the corruption that is in the world by lust.[5]

How do we live a life of godliness? By becoming partakers in the divine nature.

But how can we who are created and sinful come into communion with that which is uncreated and holy? It is impossible. Why, in the Old Testament, people were struck dead for simply touching the holy mountain! The same was true if they entered the Holy of Holies. We cannot even look upon God and live. That which is created cannot be joined with uncreated divine nature. So if Peter says the key to holiness is partaking of the divine nature, how can we have access to that nature? The Incarnation of our Lord Jesus Christ. To effect that relationship, *God had to become man.*

Now at this point, I am well aware that some will say to themselves, "But I already *know* that." You *may* know it intellectually. But let me be bold to say that if you are having daily struggles with holiness, you do not know the reality of the Incarnation—God taking on human flesh—in the manner God intended. In fact, this could be the most important section of the entire book for you. Read on attentively about the God who became man.

THE PHYSICAL GOD

Divine nature is eternal; human nature is temporal, or bound to time and space. Therefore, it would take someone both human and eternal to reconcile fallen man to God and offer eternal life.

The Second Person of the Trinity, the eternally begotten Son of God, took on our human nature in the womb of Mary. He was already sharing the divine nature from all eternity; He had no *need* to take on human nature. Because He had no need for a human nature, it was not for His own sake that He did this, "but for us men and for our salvation."[6]

Thus, out of His love for us, the Second Person of the Trinity entered the womb of the Virgin Mary and, with God the Father overshadowing the event and the Holy Spirit entering the womb of Mary as the one through whom our Lord Jesus Christ was conceived, the work of the Incarnation had begun.

We know from Luke's account of the virgin birth that all three persons of the Trinity were involved in the Incarnation. But only one of those persons took on human nature. The Son of God took humanity upon Himself and made it His own. Further, He took *all* of our humanity, except sin, because all of our humanity had been damaged by sin and death.

The ancient fathers had a saying which is helpful to us here. It was stated in the negative: "That which is not assumed is not healed."[7] Unless the Son of God assumed all of what we are as human beings (except for sin), there was no way that He would be able to fully save or fully restore us. He took on all of what we are that we might be healed. And when He did, human nature was brought into a genuine union with His divine nature. His human nature did not lose its identity and His divine nature did not lose its identity, because He remained fully God and fully man.

But what is the outcome of that union, that joining of God and man in the person of the Son of God?

It is not addition. That is, it is not a mixing or mingling of the two natures with one another. Nor is He part God and part man, for He shares fully humanity *and* deity.

It is *interpenetration*. The divine nature began, with the Incarnation, to interpenetrate the human nature of our Lord Jesus Christ in the womb of Mary, and this was true throughout His life. The great illustration which was used in the ancient church is that of the fire and the sword. Jon Braun captures it well:

> Fire has one kind of nature and iron another kind of nature quite distinct from it. Yet the heat of the fire penetrates the sword, heating it to an intense heat. The sword partakes of an aspect of the fire, its heat. However, most assuredly, the sword does not become fire. Both the fire and the sword maintain their distinct natures. Still, the sword is hot from the fire.[8]

In this illustration, the sword does not become the fire and the fire does not become the sword. Each keeps its own identity. Heat from the fire is *in* the sword just as the characteristics of divine nature (the fruit of the Spirit, godly character) interpenetrate human nature.

When our Lord was born, though He was at once wholly God and wholly man, He was not yet fully developed in His human nature. He began His life on this earth as we all do, as an infant. Make no mistake: He was sinless from the very beginning, but He had to grow up and mature as we do. Remember, He assumed everything that we are, and this included the growth process.

The Scriptures tell us that "He learned obedience from the things which He suffered."[9] He grew as a boy, as a teen-ager, as a young man, and into full adulthood. Because of this, He understands all of our weaknesses. I have a friend who used to preach a message entitled "What Jesus Was Like in College." In that particular homily, he developed the idea that there had to have been a day in the life of our Lord Jesus when he walked the streets of ancient Nazareth and noticed an appealing young maiden. For as the Scripture says, He "has been tempted in all things as we are, yet without sin."[10] Certainly, then, He was tempted by lust, just as He was by power, by greed, and all the other sins that confront us. But He never yielded; He never sinned.

In His sacrifice for us, He submitted His human nature to

death, and at that point He experienced broken communion with His Father. As Scripture tells us, He descended into hell.[11] That was no mere "spiritual" descent. And, praise God, hell could not contain Him! In fact, He spoiled the "lower earth!" It was there that He pulled down principalities and powers. And in great power and glory, He was raised from the dead and, forty days later, ascended into heaven.

Throughout this ordeal, at no time was the Son of God separated from His human nature. And He will wear His humanity *forever;* thus, today we have a *man* representing us in heaven!

It is absolutely imperative to our on-going salvation that He keep His human nature, because we could not come into communion with the Father apart from our relationship with the Son in His humanity. We need a mediator *continually,* the Son of God in His glorified humanity.

THE STATE OF THE UNION

When we are born again, we are placed by the Holy Spirit into union with the glorified humanity of our Lord Jesus Christ. It is through Him, and only through Him, that we become partakers of the divine nature. We do not go into the presence of God directly, for "No man has seen God at any time."[12] Instead, it is through the Son, the one mediator between God and man,[13] that we enter into this relationship with the eternal Triune God.

Do you see how incredibly important His incarnation is? Because He assumed everything that we are, we, through union with Him, have the power to live a godly life.

Consider three outstanding examples:

Your bodies are united with Him. ("Do you not know that your bodies are members of Christ?" 1 Cor. 6:15.)

Your minds are united with Him. ("But we have the mind of Christ" 1 Cor. 2:16.)

Your spirits are united with Him. ("But the one who joins himself to the Lord is one spirit with Him" 1 Cor. 6:17.)

Now let us enumerate what all this means to us on a practical basis.

Our bodies

Remember the potato chip ad which says, "Bet you can't eat just one"? Do you see how this slogan plays on human frailty? The ad is saying, in effect, "You do not have control over your body; therefore, you cannot effectively limit your consumption of these potato chips to merely one."

Let me say emphatically, if you have been granted everything pertaining to life and godliness and if such triviality be the will of God—yes, you *can* eat just one. You have been given control over your body because of your union with Jesus Christ.

Or, you've heard the flimsy alibi of the young man who has gone to bed with his girl friend, "But we just couldn't help it." The only ones who sin worse are the ones who believe what he is saying is true!

My brother or sister in Christ, you *can* help it. God has promised that you do have the capability, because of your union with Christ, to yield your members to righteousness. Sin is not inevitable for the person who is joined to Christ. One great statement of the Incarnation is: *You are in union with One who was tempted and said no to sin.* Therefore, through your union with Him, His indwelling Holy Spirit gives you the power to do precisely the same thing.

Let me ask you to begin living a new way: expect *not* to sin. Expect to obey the Lord and His righteousness. Count on your union with Him as you live day by day. You will be amazed at the results as you bring your body under the control of Christ.

Our minds

The Scriptures say, "Thou wilt keep him in perfect peace, whose mind is stayed on thee; because he trusteth in thee."[14] Because of our union with Jesus Christ, because we have "the mind of Christ,"[15] we are able to bring our minds under the reign of the Lord.

I recall an experience I had shortly after becoming a Christian. I was song leader for our college fraternity, and our repertoire included some songs with lyrics that would have made a sailor blush. At our "beer busts," I would be the one called upon to lead the "brothers" in a rousing medley of such songs.

For months after giving my life to Christ, at certain times the words to these songs would pass through my mind. It was as though I wanted to turn off the words but could not.

But on one particular day as I was walking to class, God said, "Turn the words of those songs over to Me."

Very consciously I prayed, "In the name of Jesus Christ, I renounce the words to these songs and the fact that they flow through my memory. Lord Jesus, remove them from my brain and somehow blot them out so I am not plagued with them again."

And do you know, the words to those songs never again automatically flowed through my brain as they once did. I never again sang them over in my mind. The "instant replay" ceased. I am certain that if I willed to go back and recapture those songs, probably I would remember quite a number of them. But I have never desired such a thing, nor has my mind ever again been the vehicle of that particular sin.

It was quite some time later—perhaps even a few years later—that I came across one of the most liberating passages I had ever seen in Scripture, having to do with our ability in Christ to take authority over our minds. In 2 Corinthians 10 the apostle Paul tells us that our warfare as physical people is essentially in the realm of the spiritual world. Then we read this statement: "We are destroying speculations and every lofty thing raised up against the knowledge of God, and we are taking every thought captive to the obedience of Christ."[16]

This is exactly what had happened to me that day back on the campus. I had volitionally brought my thoughts under the control of the Lord Jesus Christ and had experienced freedom from their control over me. As Christians, our minds do not control us; we, through Christ, control them! Hence, this business of "my mind played tricks on me" or "I just can't help thinking those bad thoughts," is no longer a legitimate excuse. For in our union with

Christ, and as partakers of the divine nature, we can know and experience a renewing of our minds!

Let me say one other thing concerning the mind of the Christian. Every so often—especially when there has been a corrective issued to a so-called Christian—this argument will be made, "Well, what I am doing is a matter of conscience. What you are saying is *your* opinion. The Lord hasn't shown that to me. And besides, you can't control what I believe. Jesus Christ is my Lord, and He has given me my own free will. *I* must do what *I* believe to be right!"

Not necessarily so.

First of all, when we surrender ourselves to Jesus Christ, we give Him *everything*—conscience and all. To say we reserve the final right to our own opinion "under His lordship" is double-talk. Was it not our Lord Jesus who, when His death was imminent, said, "Not My will, but Thine be done"?[17] Most assuredly, His conscience was surrendered to the headship of His Father. And if His, why not ours?

Secondly, since when does one person, *all by himself*, have the authority to be the final judge of God's will? From the beginning, God instructed that by the voice of two or three witnesses things shall be established. Such rationalizers will often appeal to Scripture, saying, "But I believe the Bible teaches it *this* way." And the apostle Peter retorts: "But know this first of all, that no prophecy of Scripture is a matter of one's own interpretation."[18] Thus, we must stand squarely in the mainstream of the church of God regarding the interpretation of Scripture.

Third, we are creatures of the Fall. To say my conscience is my guide is to adopt "Jiminy Cricket theology." How absurd to think that *my* conscience alone, though educated and sophisticated, possesses the ability to determine the will of God.

Some might fear that I am saying we have to check out *everything* we do with the church before we do it. That's impossible! Our lives are to be lived out under the guidance of the Holy Spirit, obeying the Lord as we go. I certainly can't ask permission for every little move I make. After all, God has given me a brain. But I am accountable to the Lord in His church, not just to my own conscience. This means I am correctable—that if while walking with Him I err, I will not blast ahead on my own, but will bend my will to God's.

And finally, the person who claims to live by his conscience will likely lie to you about other things, too. One of the first quotes on record by the father of lies was, "Hath *God* said?"[19] Adam, when confronted with his sin, said, "She [Eve] gave me from the tree, and I ate."[20] And Eve said, "The *serpent* deceived me."[21] Talk about passing the buck!

Do remember this: You and I need to take care lest we fall into similar deception. For should the tables be turned and God speak through another person to us, our temptation will be to scamper back to that same old alibi of conscience and make it our own. We, too, need to be surrendered to Christ as He rules in His *church*.

Our spirits

The Scriptures say, "The Spirit Himself bears witness with our spirit that we are children of God."[22] Let me describe what happens to our spirits by using a biblical picture.

You will remember that in the New Testament the Holy Spirit is sometimes pictured as a dove. As a matter of fact, when Jesus came up out of the water after being baptized, as recorded in the Gospels, the Holy Spirit descended upon Him as a dove. And so it is with us: the biblical norm is that we believe, are baptized, and receive the gift of the Holy Spirit.

This presupposes that before we come to faith in Christ, the Holy Spirit has not been personally present with us.

When man sinned in the Garden of Eden, the communion he had enjoyed with God was broken. Or, to put it another way, the dove left and our spirits became dead in sin.

We do not mean by this that our human spirits were dead in the sense of being annihilated. They were dead in that they were dead to the promptings of the Holy Spirit. For Paul tells us that even as pagans or unbelievers we were still led[23]—certainly not by God's Spirit, but rather by "the spirit that now is working in the sons of disobedience."[24] It is a frightening thing to be living outside of Jesus Christ.

It is only after we are brought back into union with Christ that the communion with God is reestablished and the heavenly dove once again descends on us. Then His Holy Spirit indwells us, activating our human spirits to the things of God instead of the things of the flesh. Thus, we become alive to God.[25]

HOW CAN I SAY THANKS?

What more can we say? "He who did not spare His own Son, but delivered Him up for us all, how will He not also with Him freely give us all things?"[26]

Our Lord Jesus Christ, in taking upon Himself full humanity while continuing forever also as fully God, has made it possible for *us* to be restored to full humanity. For we are united with His glorious humanity. And through Him as mediator—God and man—we become partakers of the divine nature, that we might live holy and godly lives in this present world.

It is not that He took human beings and made them superhuman. Instead, he took subhumans (sinners if you will) and restored them again to their full humanity. There is an incredible difference! A Christian is not one who is better than all the rest; he is simply one who is better than he was—through the grace and mercy of the Lord Jesus Christ!

In two later chapters, we will discuss two physical means which God has provided to effect and nourish this union. For our magnificent union with Him is sustained by two physical acts which are forever ordained by God. But first we must look at the very physical, visible priesthood in which our Lord Jesus Christ is known and adored.

But as it is now our purpose to discourse of the visible Church, let us learn, from her single title of Mother, how useful, nay, how necessary the knowledge of her is, since there is no other means of entering into life unless she conceive us in the womb and give us birth, unless she nourish us at her breasts, and, in short, keep us under her charge and government, until, divested of mortal flesh, we become like the angels.

John Calvin

7

A

NATIONAL CONSCIOUSNESS

The other evening I was reading through the newspaper, and the headline of an advertisement for a local weight-loss salon caught my attention: "IF YOU COULD LOSE WEIGHT BY YOURSELF, YOU WOULD HAVE DONE SO BY NOW."

This headline put into words something I had believed for a long time. "What incredible implications that statement has for those of us in the body of Christ," I thought. For we could say, "If you could live a holy life by yourself, you would have done so by now." Or, "If you could meet your own needs by yourself, you would have done so by now." Or, "If you could worship the Lord by yourself, you would have done so by now."

In the last chapter we discussed the fact that because the eternal Son of God became man, because He assumed everything that we are except for sin, we through union with Him become partakers of the divine nature. Thus, we are able to live out the Christian life as members of Christ, fully acceptable before the Father.

But to stop there would make our discussion of godliness incomplete. For we are also "members one of another."[1] In exhorting His people to be holy, the Lord did not mean holiness would be accomplished by people walking with Him all alone. For even that statement was spoken to the people of God, not simply to isolated, believing individuals.

Practical provision for holy living has been made through the work of our Lord Jesus Christ as we are born and placed within His body here on earth to live out that holiness with others who are redeemed. We will never be fully what God intends us to be if we simply try to relate to Him by ourselves.

THERE'S A FORD IN YOUR FUTURE

A few years back, one of my fellow elders in our home church approached me and said, "Peter, can I tell you something straightforward?"

I'm a born pessimist when it comes to welcoming a loaded question like that! But we have an up-front commitment in our church that encourages complete honesty with one another. Such honesty is only made possible because this commitment is based on the commitment which we share with Christ. So I gulped and said, "What do you have in mind?"

"You don't do enough for your children," Buddy Taylor began, with his usual air of confidence and boldness.

"What do you mean?" I asked, a bit stunned.

"Don't get me wrong," he continued. "I don't mean you don't love them. You've got about as loving a family as I've ever seen. But you need to *do more* for them. I tried to do a lot for my kids, and if I had it to do over, I'd do even more."

Buddy and Lee Taylor are in their mid-fifties and have raised three boys, all of whom are now grown and gone. When they were in their late forties, this dear couple came alive to Jesus Christ, to the reality of the Holy Spirit, and to the church. The Taylors have been close and significant friends to us, in part because they serve as very personal models to Marilyn and me as we are moving into our prime time of middle age.

"What do you have in mind, Buddy?" I asked. "Give me some specifics."

"I mean you need to do things like take them out to eat more, buy each one a cute new outfit now and then. Just something special. I don't mean spending a lot of money on them; I mean doing tangible things beyond simply *saying* that you love them or providing them with daily necessities."

Honestly, I would never have caught the deficiency he saw in my fatherhood in a million years. But Buddy was dead right. I had told my kids I loved them, I had been most generous with hugs and kisses, and I had taken many fun trips with them. But as far as buying them special things—going that extra mile—I had really been short-sighted. Unlike our heavenly Father, I was not a gift-giver.

It wasn't two or three days later that my older son, Greg, and I were driving down a country highway together on the way home from doing an errand. We passed a corn field and at the south end of that field sat an old '48 Ford. Not knowing of my conversation with Buddy a few days before, Greg commented, "Boy, I'd love to have a car like that."

It just so happened that the man was willing to sell the car, and it was in my affordable price range. Greg and I have had a great time these past three years driving that car and *slowly* fixing it up together. That '48 Ford was the first in a series of "tangibles" that I've been able to procure for my children.

A GIANT CARE PACKAGE

What kind of a church is it where the people are *governed* instead of just *advised?* For when Buddy confronted me, it was not merely to share his opinion; it was to speak a word from God to me. And I agreed that it was true.

The church *is* the government of God on the earth. It is not a club where individual Christians meet together once or twice a week. Again, the apostle Peter speaks so clearly to that issue when he says, "But you are a chosen race, a royal priesthood, *a holy nation*, a people for God's own possession, that you may proclaim the excellencies of Him who has called you out of darkness into His marvelous light."[2]

As a citizen of the United States, I answer to the government of the United States. I do not do whatever I please. The same is true for people in other countries, if those governments are worth their salt. And in the church of Jesus Christ there are continual, dynamic orders given through the Holy Spirit to the people of God, and those edicts are to be heeded and obeyed. But somehow we have lost our "national consciousness" in the church; we have degenerated into living isolated lives, deciding on our own what is or what is not God's will.

There is something interesting about modern Christians: We somehow feel that if we can learn all of the Bible verses on a given subject, or nail down the "doctrine," this is tantamount to actually *doing* what those verses or doctrines teach. For example, you can question the average Christian about what the Bible says concerning spiritual gifts. If he is well-versed in the Scriptures, he'll give you the right answers. And yet when you check to see what he is *doing*, most often it is little or nothing. But somehow, memorizing the verses on spiritual gifts has given him some sort of assurance that he is being "biblical" in his view, even though he may not really want to experience the gifts of the Spirit.

And in our view of the church in general, it is much the same story. We read and memorize verses telling us that the church is a holy nation, but it never occurs to us to be under that nation's government. We "see it as spiritual"; we do not flesh it out. We are content merely with a holy nation in doctrine. We do not care to have a physical, visible, locatable holy nation to which we actually report and are accountable.

A one-evening skimming through the New Testament will demonstrate the awesome presence of the church operating as a government or nation over the people of God. For example, Paul writes, "If any one thinks he is a prophet or spiritual, let him recognize that the things which I write to you are the Lord's commandment."[3] Did Paul mean that what he said was to be actually carried out in the church? I'll guarantee you he did!

Or, where Paul writes, "And if anyone does not obey our instruction in this letter, take special note of that man and do not associate with him, so that he may be put to shame. And yet do not regard him as an enemy, but admonish him as a brother."[4]

Did those recipients of his letter simply believe that exhortation to be "inerrantly inspired," or did they also carry it out and dissociate themselves from those who disobeyed Paul! And if they did carry it out, why can't we do the same? Why is it easier to join a church than to join a country club? When is the church going to start governing and caring again?

To better understand why the church has lost sight of its role as a nation and a government, let us consider the following:

The culture

Basically, we are taught to do things for ourselves from the cradle to the grave. Our folk heroes, be they the Lone Ranger, Zorro, Archie Bunker, or Barnaby Jones, basically get the job done all by themselves. The "nobody's gonna tell me what to do" attitude of society has certainly left its mark upon the church. A Protestant church that tells its people what to do is a church which everyone leaves to look for a new one. We simply do not want our lives interfered with, and thus we are happy when we sit under teaching which says the government of God is not physically present nor actively and dynamically at work. We want Christ and His kingdom working in our own, private hearts—not in our midst.

The revolt against liberalism and/or churchianity

Many who have come out of backgrounds where the power of the gospel has been denied, or out of the "dead-church doldrums," and have been converted to Christ overstate things—probably without even realizing it. In the contemporary scene, one often hears statements such as, "Praise the Lord! After years of sitting in church, He has freed me from that bondage and showed me all I need is Jesus." In their zeal to exalt the Lord, and because of their previous disappointments with the church, they have opted for a nonexistent brand of Christianity which enthusiastically proclaims, "Seek ye first the kingdom of God,"[5] but denies that there is any visible reign of Christ through the church. The kingdom becomes only future, and you have a band of believers which enthusiastically points to the *king*, but completely misses the *dom*.

The rise of the parachurch movement

You can read the Scriptures from now until Christ returns and not find one single passage to substantiate any other movement of

God besides Israel in the Old Testament and the church in the New. Nonetheless, independent Christian organizations continue to flourish numerically and economically as they capture the imaginations of visionary believers with their incredible plans for mission and claims of success.

But the very gospel which they proclaim stops short of what God is after for His people. The convert—instead of being born into a legitimate, functioning, physical family in which there is a commitment to care, to worship, and to keep watch over its members' souls—is ushered into a relationship with Jesus Christ which is invisible and mental. There is no sense of true community, of sacrament, of answerability to godly elders under whom the person becomes nurtured. It is as though we have removed plants from the garden and set them one by one in pots away from the rest.

Having said that, however, there is another side to the story. It is no secret to any of us that in the last several decades an enormous segment of the church has quit preaching and teaching a personal union with Jesus Christ. For them, salvation consists of being in the church; it does not include the element of personal faith or response. And this spiritual vacuum is, in large part, what has given birth and sustenance to the parachurch emphasis. So, in a very real way, the church asked for it, becoming cold and ritualistic. Now these groups are doing an expensive end run on the church.

Today, there are hundreds of agencies claiming to be "arms of the church" (has the whole body become an arm?!) which have no real connection to her at all. Some of these have multi-million-dollar budgets; money which should be going into the house of God is being used for religious private enterprise. And manpower! Where are the lion's share of the leaders, communicators, teachers, and administrators today? They're the "executives" of the parachurch conglomerates.

In the midst of all this, to regain a biblical ecclesiology, to reestablish the church as the locus of God's presence, becomes a herculean task.

I do have a proposal, though—a place to begin.

Throughout church history, there has been a proper parachurch movement. Often, when a particular emphasis had been overlooked in the church, a group of its people would unite— under church authority, not outside of it—and form *holy orders.* They would concentrate on regaining that needed element in the body of Christ. Saint Francis of Assisi and his Franciscan order are a noted historical example. What I propose is that movements such as Young Life, Youth for Christ, Inter-Varsity, Campus Crusade for Christ, Christian Women's Club, Full Gospel Businessmen's Committee, and all the rest—if they are what they say they are, an arm of the church—submit their work to the authority of a solid church body in the biblical tradition.

For years, I have heard several of the leaders of parachurch groups make this statement: "We exist only because the church has not done the job. So we are here to serve. We pray for the day when our organization no longer needs to exist."

That day has come. There are ample numbers of denominations with the same sort of evangelical fervor espoused by the para-church organizations. And what a testimony it would be to the unity of the body of Christ to see people willing to lose their special identities and come back under the auspices of the church of Jesus Christ once again.

Perhaps one of the most effective parachurch movements of the 1960s was the Christian World Liberation Front (CWLF) which was begun in 1965 to reach the counter-culture people in Berkeley, California. Jack Sparks, who began the organization, had been an associate professor first at Colorado State, then at Penn State. He shed his Brooks Brothers suits, donned work shirts and blue jeans, grew a beard, and, with many enthusiastic associates, had an enormous effect on the radical Berkeley scene. People were brought to Christ, there was a real attempt toward community, the homeless and rejected were given food and shelter, and the message of the gospel was spoken in the language of the people.

But even more impressive than all of this was Jack's response to the waning of the counter-culture. By the early 1970s, it was no longer "in" to be a hippie, the revolutionaries got tired of revolting, and many radicals who remained in town got jobs and melted into society. Thus, there was no real reason for CWLF to continue. So

Jack closed her down! And today many of those people are a part of Redeemer King Church near Berkeley which sprang up as a result. My point is—*it can be done.* One of Jack's greatest personal struggles was the monetary one. He had a sizeable mailing list of loyal, giving constituents. He could have cooked up an alternate reason to exist and kept going indefinitely. Instead, through no small sacrifice and tension, Jack Sparks chose the lordship of Jesus Christ in the church over having a "personal ministry" and a comfortable future on the outside.

The vacuum of authority in the church; the diminishing status of church leadership

We evangelicals are a strange group! We have certain dogmatic views, but there is an inbred hesitancy to "get involved" and enforce those views in the lives of errant sheep and shepherds. For example, our view on morality. From time to time, a Christian will fall into sexual immorality or will be dishonest in business practices. Instead of getting involved in that person's life with care and discipline, we often just add his or her name to a prayer list. We have the idea that God will take care of everyone without calling on His people to carry out His mercy and justice. Sort of a "be warmed and fed" view.

This passivity is a result of lack of authority in the evangelical church. Most everything is local and autonomous. Nobody is there to correct an evangelical pastor when he is out of line, because there are no bishops in evangelicalism. In fact, the movement prides itself in having none. *Christianity Today* is the closest thing there is to a central clearing house. But what evangelicalism fails to realize is that lack of spiritual authority will cost it its life.

It is likewise disturbing that the height of success within evangelicalism is when a pastor "graduates" to being a conference speaker, or a full-time author and lecturer, or perhaps even to the presidency of a parachurch organization. The carrot is being the newest personality on the speakers' circuit.

Since when is there *any* higher calling than being a shepherd of the flock of Jesus Christ? Personally, having gone from being a full-time author and speaker back into the church as a shepherd, I will say that shepherding the flock is ten times tougher. To simply pop from town to town handing out "new birth" certificates to all who will pray a little prayer absolutely absolves the speaker of any responsibility for the new convert. These are "hit-men for Jesus," flitting from conference to conference, from banquet to banquet, sowing the seed gleefully while establishing and promoting nothing permanent. Honestly, what is the difference between this sort of practice and the wholesale fathering of children from town to town with women you don't even know? This "alley-cat evangelism" has to cease.

REDISCOVERING A VITAL CHURCH

But the question still remains: What about the future of the church itself? What must be done to get things back in order there?

I believe there are three primary areas in the life of the church which need to be changed. Without these three components being believed and practiced, the vital life which the church once knew in its early centuries will never be regained.

A common biblical doctrine

The Roman Catholic church claims to hold to and teach the New Testament faith. The Baptist church says that it teaches the doctrine of the Bible. The Lutherans say they do. Ditto for the Presbyterians. And even certain cults such as The Way, International, the Local Church of Witness Lee, and Jehovah's Witnesses claim that they teach the true biblical doctrine. How do we go about sorting these things out?

As we noted earlier, the apostle Peter exhorted, "But know this first of all, that no prophecy of Scripture is a matter of one's own interpretation."[6] As individuals we simply are not to decide for ourselves what the Scriptures mean. And who better could comment on that weakness than Peter! For as we have recorded in Galatians 2, this is exactly the trap into which he fell, teaching the early Gentile Christians that they should obey the laws of Judaism.

It is here that the witness of apostles, prophets, evangelists, pastors and teachers, and appointed leaders throughout the history of the church is so imperative. For there is a discernible mainstream of consistent interpretation down through the ages. The apostles' doctrine is present in the gospels, the epistles, in the great church creeds (such as the Apostles' Creed, the Nicene Creed, the Chalcedon Creed); it is echoed by the Reformers, the Puritan fathers, and is to be believed in the church today. Thus, when we use the term "apostolic doctrine," we mean those truths which were commonly held and believed by men of God throughout the history of the church, based upon the Holy Scriptures.

In the modern church with its many-faceted expressions and beliefs, the thought of embracing a *common faith* is indeed mind-boggling. It means that virtually all of us will have to repent and change in order to make such adjustments. But it is comforting to realize that those adjustments which must be made will move us toward the centrality of truth and not away from it. The ancient faith, the apostolic doctrine, must once again be believed and practiced if the church is to emerge from its captivity and return to spiritual health.

A common liturgy

Interestingly, the word *liturgy* comes from two Greek words: *laos*, meaning people, and *ergos*, meaning to work. (Note the physicalness of the word!) A more colloquial definition of the word would be "the way people commonly do things." As a matter of fact, "life style" is not all that bad as a supplemental definition for liturgy.

For some, the word *liturgy* holds a very negative connotation. We have been told that liturgy boxes in the work of the Holy Spirit. Bad liturgy does; true liturgy does not. It's a word we need to like again.

And there is something you must understand: *All* churches have liturgies. You may protest and say, "But I'm a member of a Pentecostal church which is free from liturgy to worship the Lord in the Spirit." To which I would reply, "If you really worship the Lord in the Spirit, He will have given you a liturgy." Those who are Pentecostal, or who have visited a Pentecostal church from time to time, will know exactly what I mean. There is a predictable pattern in these services. The songs are sung at the same time; the prayers are offered in the same time slot. As a matter of fact, people are even slain in the Spirit at roughly the same point in the service each Sunday. There is no getting around it: a pattern develops in a short space of time. Life demands it.

In the ancient church, liturgy is discernible from the very start. One of the earliest records we have of common liturgy is called Justin's Liturgy, based upon an account of church worship that Justin Martyr wrote in the second century. It is parallel in many ways to the synagogue worship and to the ancient Jewish temple worship. (I have devoted an entire chapter to "The Physical Side of Worship" and will specifically include this ancient liturgy of the church.)

Just as we do not interpret the Bible in any way we please, so we do not do our own thing in worship. There is a proper liturgy. And though it would take an entire book to prove it, if the church of Jesus Christ is ever going to know a godly unity again, she will need to come to agreement on a basic liturgy.

A biblical government

Within the broad scope of Christendom, there are as many forms of church government in the various church bodies as there are opinions on doctrines and worship, and all believe theirs is the biblical one. But did you know that there is one, discernible form of government which has been practiced throughout church history? In recent centuries it has often been prostituted and made pompous, but nonetheless, there is a visible government that is common within the historic church. And until this government is once again instituted and practiced in the church, the people of God will never know the full health and vitality that was so apparent at the beginning. It goes without saying that in order to do this, much crow will need to be eaten in the area of church government, just as in the areas of doctrine and worship.

I hate to say this in front of all my Baptist friends, but you can trace bishops right back into the New Testament! Thankfully, the modern Protestant church has held onto elders and deacons and, of course, the laity or the people of God. But it has largely scrapped the office of bishop. And without this office, the church will never run on all its cylinders.

As early as Acts 1, after Judas had apostasized and committed suicide, Peter reminded the other ten apostles of the scriptural command concerning the vacancy, "his bishoprick let another take."[7] At the Jerusalem council, described in Acts 15, though Peter, the acknowledged head of the Twelve, was present, James, the bishop of Jerusalem, ran the meeting.

Ignatius of Antioch was consecrated bishop in that city about A.D. 70 , and he served there forty years. Friends, that was in *Bible times!* We know of only two of the Twelve who had departed the earth at that time, James and Peter. Though it is certainly possible some of the others were deceased, it is likewise probable that at least half of them were still alive. Of course, according to tradition, the beloved John lived until the mid or late nineties. And if the Twelve had not wanted bishops—indeed, if they had not appointed them—those "sons of thunder" would have put a stop to them in a hurry! So you have the bishopric established from the very beginning of the church.

By the second century, the apostolic ministry was far less itinerant than in the first century. After all, the church had grown significantly, and those in the apostolic office and tradition were appointed to look over specific metropolitan areas rather than just traveling from place to place. Thus, by the early second century, bishops were present in every major center where the church existed. In fact, now the bishops were sending out apostolic workers to plant and build new churches, and these workers were called *missionaries!*

On this basis, then, four specific orders or offices came to be recognized very early in the church: (a) bishop, (b) presbyter, elder, or priest, (c) deacon, and (d) laity, the people of God. Each of these orders functioned actively, and the government of the church was clearly delineated.

In order for the church to return to the health that it once knew, proper government must again be instituted and must function. Given our present condition, it would take a miracle for this to happen. But our God is a God of miracles; nothing is too hard for

Him. We cannot simply let it wait for another day or time; biblical, authoritative church government must be called for in our day.

You cannot have healthy, thriving Christians without a healthy, thriving church, any more than you can grow hearty vegetables in an uncultivated, unworked garden; or grow good fruit on a rotten tree; or draw sweet water from a sour well. Obey God and stand with Him in your submission to the church, instead of flowing with the times, in and out of the various programs of men.

Peter and John supplied what was lacking; prayer was made for the baptized, the hand laid upon them, the Holy Spirit was-invoked and was poured upon them. The same practice is observed among us now; those baptized in the Church are brought to the officers of the Church and by our prayer and imposition of the hand they obtain the Holy Spirit and are perfected by the seal of the Lord.

Cyprian

8

THE
WATER AND THE SPIRIT

There is a physical side of being spiritual which is so obvious it is easy to overlook. Furthermore, the opinions of men surrounding it are so emotionally charged that they have been a source of nasty division within the church, especially in the last four hundred years.

For that reason, many modern Christians are intimidated by the subject of holy baptism and are uncomfortable when it is discussed in a group situation where they are uncertain what those present believe concerning it. In fact, it is almost considered "cool" not to have a settled opinion concerning baptism. There are some churches today who take pride in being open to all modes of baptism and to a wide range of definitions as to what that baptism really means. So, to come right out and say there has been a commonly held view of baptism in the church for centuries stands against the modern tide of trendy Christianity and is also a bit unsettling to people who have thought the doctrine of baptism was virtually up for grabs.

In this chapter, I will discuss the view and practice of baptism in the early church. Then we will look carefully at the New Testament passages that formed the basis for the practice of baptism in the church. Finally, we will talk practically about baptism of God's people today.

Someone has referred to baptism as "the waters which divide." That simply is not so. Baptism is not a source of division in the church and it never will be; the heterodox views which men have held concerning baptism are the source of division.

Time was, I'd get the spiritual blues when this passage of Scripture was read: "There is one body and one Spirit, just as also you were called in one hope of your calling; one Lord, one faith, one baptism, one God and Father of all who is over all and through all and in all."[1] If you consider that passage strictly from the vantage point of twentieth-century Christendom, it certainly seems that this oneness would be impossible to achieve. Some have gone so far as to dismiss this passage as "idealism."

But even a brief study of the early centuries of the church shows that indeed there was a view of baptism which was commonly held by the majority of Christians everywhere. As you read through the ancient fathers of the church, you become aware that they recognized three major components in the sacrament of baptism: (1) belief in the Father, Son, and Holy Spirit with renunciation of the enemy, (2) the actual immersion in the water in the name of the Father, the Son, and the Holy Spirit, and (3) the "chrismation" or laying on of hands whereby the newly baptized believer received the fullness and gifts of the Holy Spirit. Note this threefold progression well, for it is echoed with marked clarity throughout the Gospels, the Acts, the Epistles, and virtually the entire history of the church.

Of course, the source for this progression is the baptism of our Lord Jesus Christ Himself, referred to by all four of the Gospel writers. You will recall how Jesus was baptized by John and, upon coming up out of the water, received the Holy Spirit in the form of a dove. Upon this sequence of events, the ancient baptismal liturgies were formed.

Note this basic pattern, for example, in the following sections from the writings of Cyril of Jerusalem in the fourth century. This work is especially important because it was from a basic catechetical or teaching guide which Cyril had prepared:

> You stand facing west . . . because west is the region of visible darkness, and Satan is darkness and his domain is darkness. . . .

You say, "I renounce thee, Satan, and all thy works. . . ."

. . . You turn from the west to the east, the region of light. And you were told to say, "I believe in the Father, and in the Son, and in the Holy Ghost, and in one baptism of repentence."

. . . You took off your clothes: this was a symbol of stripping off the old man . . . you were anointed with exorcized oil. . . . After this you were led by the hand to the holy pool of divine baptism . . . and each of you was asked if he believed in the Name of the Father, and of the Son, and of the Holy Ghost. And you made that saving confession; you descended into the water and came up again three times. . . . In the very same moment you died and were born.

. . . When you came up from the pool of holy streams, chrism (the gifting of the Spirit) was given you, an emblem of the anointing of Christ. This is the Holy Spirit. . . .[2]

Among the abundance of other ancient commentaries on baptism, there is a short statement that was written in the second century as part of what is known as the *Didache*, literally "The Teaching," a Greek handbook of instruction in morals and church order. Here, in part, is what is said on baptism.

Baptize in the name of the Father and of the Son and of the Holy Spirit in running water. But if you do not have running water, use what is available. And if you cannot do it in cold water, use warm. But if you have neither, pour water on the head three times—in the name of the Father, Son and Holy Spirit.[3]

THE BIRTHDAY OF THE CHURCH

With the baptism of the Lord Jesus as the pattern,[4] it is no surprise that on the day of Pentecost, after Peter had preached his first sermon, when the people who heard asked what they must do, Peter replied, "Repent, and let each of you be baptized in the name of Jesus Christ for the forgiveness of your sins; and you shall receive the gift of the Holy Spirit."[5] Why would the apostle give such an answer? Because it is in baptism that our faith in Jesus Christ is effected before God and man.

This passage, and others we shall consider throughout the New Testament, is an enigma to those who have taught or been taught that *all* God wants us to do to be saved is to express faith in Jesus Christ. There is no question that we are justified by faith and that by believing we have life through His name. But mark it well:

the Scriptures consistently teach, and the historic church has continually confessed and believed, that there is a physical side of
being born again. For our Lord Himself instructed us, "Unless one
is born of water and the Spirit, he cannot enter into the kingdom of
God."[6] Thus, the ancients believed water baptism to be the act in
which the transaction of the conversion of the heart was made.

THE MODERN MEANS

If you happen to be from a "just ask Jesus into your heart"
background, may I remind you that your style of salvation also has a
physical side. Do any of these patterns sound familiar to you?

"This morning, if you are willing to open your life to Jesus
Christ and receive Him as your Savior, I'm going to ask you to
step out into the aisle right now from where you are seated
and come down front. Give your right hand to the pastor, and
in doing so you will say to him, 'This morning I am choosing to
give my heart to the Lord.'" That is *basic altar-call liturgy.*

or,

"You boys and girls have been here at camp all week, and
you've heard over and over again the claims that Jesus Christ
has on your life. Tonight is our last evening together. We've
asked you to come down here to the bonfire and to reflect
upon what you have seen and heard these days. If you have
given your heart to Christ this week, or if you would like to do
so tonight, there is a box of small wooden sticks here at the
front of the circle. To demonstrate your faith, I'm going to ask
you to come one by one and take a stick and throw it into the
fire, symbolizing your decision to follow the Lord." This is a
common *summer-camp liturgy.*

or,

"Hey, listen. Do you sense that Christ is standing at the
door of your life wanting to come in? Is there any reason you
couldn't bow your head in prayer right now and ask Him to
take over your life? You can pray something like this: 'Dear
God, I know I'm sinful and in need of a Savior. Today, I'd like

to ask you . . ." And this is the *pray-with-me liturgy*, common to many who are engaged in personal evangelism.

These methods (and others a bit bizarre, such as a listener at home being asked to place his hands on top of the radio or television set) are practiced quite widely in fundamental and evangelical circles.

And you know what? Physical manifestations such as these are significantly better than simply asking the person to exercise faith in his heart and not present a vehicle through which to manifest that faith. There is something about going forward, or throwing a stick in the fire, or praying a prayer that confirms in our hearts and minds that we have done something or that there has been a definite point in time at which a spiritual transaction has taken place. Certainly most Christians agree that some sort of public demonstration is helpful, else why would these things be practiced so broadly?

THE NORMAL MEANS

I am not against going forward or praying—or standing on your head, if that is what one is to do to come to Christ. My only question is, why have we gotten away from *God's normal means* through which our salvation is enacted? Is it because most attempts to gain converts today do not operate under the church? And why do some who name the name of Christ balk with such fearful and impassioned moans at the idea that water baptism is that place where God has chosen to transact our coming by faith into union with the Lord Jesus Christ and His church? Do they seek a better way than that revealed in Scripture?

Not only is water baptism biblical, as shown by the obedience of Christ and the preaching and practice of Peter, but it is also far and away the best physical picture to show what really takes place in the new birth. Paul writes, "Therefore we have been buried with Him through baptism into death, in order that as Christ was raised from the dead through the glory of the Father, so we too might walk in newness of life."[7]

I'll tell you, unless we return to the practice of baptism in the church as the physical vehicle through which our union with Christ is effected, our theology of the new birth will continue to get worse and worse! For the physical form of a truth is the way that truth is perceived. And it stands to reason that God, who created us as physical people, would in His gracious wisdom give us a visible means to express new life in His Son. To ignore or degrade water baptism is to stand in disobedience against God, the Holy Scriptures, and the church.

GAINING CITIZENSHIP

And there's something else at stake here, too. I do not have the authority all by myself to make the choice of whether or not I want to be a Christian. Salvation has never been unilateral! To say I make the choice *alone* is a denial both of the doctrine of divine election and of the fact that the church of Jesus Christ, that one holy nation, is active in such matters. You will remember the words of our Lord to His apostles, "If you forgive the sins of any, their sins have been forgiven them; if you retain the sins of any, they have been retained."[8] This authority is deposited in and passed on through the church.

Say that I have recently come to America from a foreign country and want to establish my home in the United States. I absolutely cannot grant *myself* citizenship. In fact, unless I am *made* a citizen, there is a term to describe me: I am an *illegal alien!* I must apply for citizenship, must be recognized by the government as a desirable candidate, and must then swear before a judge that I will obey the Constitution and uphold the laws of the land. It is *he* who declares me a citizen, not *me.*

Someone may object, "But that is the world's way of doing things." It sure is! And do you know where our government got that practice? The same place it got the idea for the executive, legislative, and judicial "orders" of government: church polity.

Jesus said, "You did not choose Me, but I chose you, and appointed you."[9] The men He sent out built the church which is His body, the outpost of His heavenly government on earth. And the church is involved in the affairs of Jesus Christ. You simply do not come in all by yourself, even though personal faith is a requisite. You are recognized and brought in by the Holy Spirit through the waters of baptism in the church here on the earth: you believe, are baptized, and are saved!

THE SAMARITAN EXPANSION

There's not a clearer passage about how all these things work together than the one in Acts 8, where Philip, an evangelist, goes into Samaria with the word of God. "But when they believed Philip preaching the good news about the kingdom of God and the name of Jesus Christ, they were being baptized, men and women alike."[10]

Here are phases one and two of the baptismal liturgy. First of all, the people responded to Philip's message by placing their *trust* in the Lord Jesus Christ as the author and finisher of their salvation. Then they are recognized as ones who believe, are *baptized* in water, and are brought into union with Christ and His church.

But they have not experienced phase three yet. That is, the people have believed and been baptized, but it's not until a short time later that they are filled with the Holy Spirit, or *chrismated*. Since Samaria was "virgin territory" populated with people who were part Jew and part Gentile, and since the apostles were the ones through whom the Holy Spirit was initially ministered in the church, it remained for them to come to Samaria to complete the work that the Lord, through Philip, had begun. And thus the Scriptures say,

> Now when the apostles in Jerusalem heard that Samaria had received the word of God, they sent them Peter and John, who came down and prayed for them, that they might receive the Holy Spirit. For He had not yet fallen upon any of them; they had simply been baptized in the name of the Lord Jesus. Then they began laying their hands on them, and they were receiving the Holy Spirit.[11]

We need to get the baptism of the Holy Spirit back into the church where it belongs, rather than leaving it to be administered at summer camps or Holiday Inn meeting halls on Saturday nights. It is my personal opinion that because the church has quit preaching the fullness of the Holy Spirit, God has allowed this truth to be exported. But, as with evangelism, how sorely we need to get things back into perspective once again. It is encouraging to me to know that many pastors and bishops who know the Lord are once again calling for the laying on of hands in the church, that God's people may receive the fullness and the gifts of the Holy Spirit.

When the work of the Holy Spirit is brought again into the believing church, things come out far more balanced, decent, and orderly than they do at some free-for-all praise session. I thank the Lord for the way He has worked in the charismatic movement to get our attention back on the Third Person of the Trinity once again. But the charismatic movement needs to move back into the visible church, to get on with the whole program of God and the other two persons of the Godhead, rather than to continue as a spiritual specialty house, doing business outside the holy nation.

CREATIVITY AT CORNELIUS'S HOUSE

Even though the baptismal liturgy continues on in Acts, things happened a bit differently with Cornelius. Throughout the history of Israel, the Gentiles were seen as the "dogs," the unclean ones in the sight of the Jews. Therefore, God decided to do something spectacular and creative so Peter and the others would truly believe that the gospel had taken hold in the hearts of the Gentiles as well.

And if I had been Peter, I would have wanted events to progress just exactly the way they did. For I have the feeling I would have been too cowardly to advocate the bringing of this Gentile household into the church had not something supernatural happened to convince me that God had indeed opened the door to those Gentiles. Let's join the text as Peter is speaking.

> "Of Him all the prophets bear witness that through His name every one who believes in Him has received forgiveness of sins." While Peter was still speaking these words, the Holy Spirit fell upon all those who were listening to the message. And all the circumcised believers who had come with Peter were amazed, because the gift of the Holy Spirit had been poured out upon the Gentiles also. For they were hearing them speaking with tongues and exalting God. Then Peter answered, "Surely no one can refuse the water for these to be baptized who have received the Holy Spirit just as we did, can he?"[12]

What an amazing story. The apostle Peter, not known for his

brevity, was yet to finish his remarks when the Holy Spirit, "did a number" on Cornelius and his household. But what was Peter's immediate response as he saw the Spirit of God outwardly manifested in these people's lives? Of course! "It's time for baptism to seal what God has done." Thus, these Gentiles, just like their Jewish predecessors who had embraced the Messiah, were brought into union with the Lord Jesus and were recognized through Peter's authority (and later by agreement of the church at Jerusalem[13]) as part of the church.

There's an important lesson we must learn from this event. That is, you cannot always predict the way God is going to work. Though certainly we would recognize the consistency of believing, being baptized, and being filled with the Holy Spirit, even today there are times when God chooses to do something creative in the hearts of certain of His people. What we need to be released from, however, is the mentality that believes God—or His people—*always* has to be creative.

In our day, the word "tradition" has fallen on hard times. Many modern Christians despise the word, using as their proof text, "See to it that no one takes you captive through philosophy and empty deception, according to the tradition of men . . . rather than according to Christ."[14] This refers to *man-made traditions*, such as the ones we discussed earlier (going forward, praying, raising a hand), used as substitutes for baptism in bringing people into union with Christ. But there are also *godly traditions*, such as baptism and communion, which He has placed in the church. This is why Paul said, "So then, brethren, stand firm and *hold to the traditions* which you were taught, whether by word of mouth or by letter from us."[15]

We must obey the Lord and practice the traditions He has set in the church, using them gratefully, rather than murmuring, "We'll fall into formalism if we do so."

There is no contradiction between living by godly tradition and walking in the freshness of the Holy Spirit. It is not a question of either/or. We need both the water and the Spirit—badly!

FROM JOHN TO JESUS

To me, one of the most fascinating passages in the whole New Testament concerning water baptism and the indwelling of the Holy Spirit is found in Acts 19. In fact, it's a downright humorous section of Scripture. It's one of those places where some people who have a habit of underlining Bible verses don't do any underlining!

It is in places like Acts 19 that we are so grateful for the knowledge of the traditional baptismal form. For if you see the baptism of our Lord Jesus back in the gospels as the basic way baptism in the water and the Holy Spirit is to be practiced, then Acts 19 makes all the sense in the world. But if you isolate this passage and try to make it normal for all believers, not only do you completely ignore the testimony of the historic church and apostolic tradition, but you also frustrate the myriads of Christians whose experiences just will not fit into this particular mold. And believe it or not, Acts 19 is the best argument in Scripture that a baptismal liturgy had already been established by Paul's day!

> And it came about that while Apollos was at Corinth, Paul having passed through the upper country came to Ephesus, and found some disciples, and he said to them, "Did you receive the Holy Spirit when you believed?" And they said to him, "No, we have not even heard whether there is a Holy Spirit." And he said, "Into what then were you baptized?" And they said, "Into John's baptism." And Paul said, "John baptized with the baptism of repentance, telling the people to believe in Him who was coming after him, that is, in Jesus." And when they heard this, they were baptized in the name of the Lord Jesus. And when Paul had laid his hands upon them, the Holy Spirit came on them, and they began speaking with tongues and prophesying.[16]

What was it about these disciples that prompted Paul to ask if they had received the Holy Spirit? Did Paul simply discern that these men did not possess the Spirit in His fullness? I admit, I have often wondered!

At any rate, their answer to the question was, "*Who?*" They had never even heard of the Holy Spirit!

Note Paul's immediate response: "Into what then were you

baptized?" *If water baptism were not that means of grace through which God normally administered the Holy Spirit, why on earth would Paul ask such a question?* It would make no sense at all. The fact of the matter is, the apostles had been practicing and teaching since A.D 33 that salvation in Jesus Christ comes as we are baptized and receive the gift of the Holy Spirit. These ambassadors had taken literally their Lord's command, "Go therefore and make disciples of all nations, baptizing them in the name of the Father and the Son and the Holy Spirit, teaching them to observe all that I commanded you."[17] There is water in the Great Commission!

So what did Paul do with the folks in Acts 19? He baptized them in water, laid his hands on them, and they received the Holy Spirit, with tongues and prophecy.

WHAT'S YOUR PATTERN?

Just as in the early days of the church God sometimes brought people into His kingdom in an unusual way, so today He gives great grace to receive us where we are en route to once again establishing church order. The important thing is that before it's all over, we have believed in the Lord Jesus Christ, have been baptized in the church, and have received the gift of the Holy Spirit—that we have been "buried with Him through baptism."[18]

In my own case, I was baptized as an infant, came to a vital faith in Jesus Christ while a college student, and a few months later experienced the fullness of the Holy Spirit. But now, as I serve the Lord in His church, it is so good to be able to honor once again that ancient progression modeled by our Lord Jesus, in which people are brought to Christ in faith through baptism and then through the laying on of hands in the church receive the fullness of the Holy Spirit.

If you are one who has "accepted Jesus Christ all on your own," the last thing in the world I want to do is to say that your faith was not valid. On the other hand, I would be unfair if I did not exhort you to submit yourself to the authority of the Lord in His church where the word of God thrives in reality and power. Do not stop short of the fullness God has for you in the physical act of baptism and in receiving the gifts the Holy Spirit has for you.

How good and how "right" it is for us to recognize the physical aspects of God's power and to embrace the order which He seeks to bring about in all of our lives.

I urge you therefore, brethren, by the mercies of God, to present your bodies a living and holy sacrifice, acceptable to God, which is your spiritual service of worship.

Paul to the Romans

9

THE PHYSICAL SIDE OF WORSHIP

In my travels around the country, I have the opportunity to talk with countless Christians from every imaginable church background. A common complaint I hear over and over again is, "I just don't get anything out of worship."

Often that statement is accompanied by another: "Our pastor is the best Bible teacher I have ever heard. When that man opens the Scriptures, I really learn. But our church has no sense of worship." There almost appears to be a pattern: the churches that are strongest on the preaching of the Scriptures are often the weakest when it comes to worshiping and giving praise to the Lord.

People say they feel like bystanders. In most church worship services there is only one man who gets a workout—the minister. Altogether too many Roman Catholic, Orthodox, Anglican, and Protestant churches have been consistently successful in developing congregations of onlookers.

By contrast, as we march back into the history of the nation Israel, we find that worship there was an active event. And talk about physical! Why, there was dancing, clapping, processioning, singing, shouting, and all the rest. Even in her apostasy, Israel seems to have been more alive in the worship of the Lord than most contemporary Christian churches. The early church picked up this same tradition of worship, involving both the body and the soul, and practiced it from the very beginning.

AN ORDER FOR WORSHIP

I would like to take you through a typical worship service in the ancient assembly. And as I do this, I want you to pay special attention to the physical side of spiritual worship. For as these people were alive in the Lord, they certainly held nothing back in manifesting their praise and worship to God in very physical ways.

The earliest account giving a substantial picture of ancient worship comes from the well-known apologist, Justin Martyr, who lived and wrote in the second century A.D. In his account of Christian worship written primarily for those outside the church, Justin gives the following description of what went on at the Eucharist, or Holy Communion.

> At the conclusion of the prayers we greet one another with a kiss. Then, bread and a chalice containing wine mixed with water are presented to the one presiding over the brethren. He takes them (the bread and wine) and offers praise and glory to the Father of all, through the name of the Son and of the Holy Spirit, and recites lengthy prayers of thanksgiving to God in the name of those to whom he granted such favors. At the end of these prayers and thanksgiving, all present express their approval by saying "amen." This Hebrew word, amen, means "so be it" and when he who presides has celebrated the Eucharist, they whom we call deacons permit each one present to partake of the Eucharistic bread and wine and water; and they carry it also to the absentees.[1]

By the early third century, especially through the writings of Hippolytus, we gain a clearer picture of exactly how the liturgy of worship in the ancient church progressed. It was divided into two basic segments: the *public worship* (called the *synaxis*), centered primarily in the preaching of the Word; and the *Eucharist*, with the focal point being the worship of God around the table of the Lord.

Thus, should the church at Antioch in, say, A.D. 220 have had a printed bulletin, it would have looked something like this:

Public Worship (Synaxis)

Opening Greeting
   Minister: *The Lord be with you.*
   People: *And with your spirit.*
Reading of the Scriptures
   (Sections from the Psalms, the Law and the Prophets, and what we
   know today as the Gospels and the Epistles) interspersed with:
Hymnody (or singing of hymns)
Sermon (called the Homily)
Dismissals (with the blessing)
   of those not a part of the church (the seekers), the learners (the
   catechumens), and those under discipline (the penitents)
Intercessory Prayers
The Collect

Eucharist

Greeting and Response
Kiss of Peace
Offertory (the bringing of the bread and wine)
Thanksgiving Prayer
Breaking of the Bread
Eating and Drinking
Benediction

As we consider this "order of worship," you will not only see
the primacy of the physical aspects of worship, but you will also
gain insight into how worship could be strengthened today.

The people of God have always viewed worship as a *proces-*
sion. (In Chapter 10, "Table Talk," I will establish this biblically,
for both Israel and the church.) They have gone *from* somewhere
to somewhere. In the Old Covenant they proceeded from their
homes and the workaday world, out into the streets of the city, up
toward the temple—the dwelling place of God—and they drew
near to Him to participate in worshiping Him with His people. In
the church, that same basic procession occurs, although we are
talking about a temple not made with hands. In fact, if you are from
a liturgical church background, you will recall the "processional" to
open your service. In procession, "the saints go marching in" to the
presence of God!

THE READING OF SCRIPTURES

After the ancient worship was begun with the greeting and
response, the people turned their attention towards the public

reading of the Scriptures. In the early church, as well as in Israel, certain persons were actually designated and trained for the reading of the Scripture. Remember when Jesus said parenthetically, "Let the reader understand"?[2] He referred there not to the individual Bible reader, but to the public reader in the synagogue. The reader was to make the holy writings as alive as possible to the ears of the people, and to do so, he himself needed to have a clear understanding of what he was reading.

Don't forget, people did not carry their Bibles with them to worship either in Israel or for approximately the first 1700 years of the church! For until the invention of the printing press, only the priests and the rich had personal copies of the Scriptures. The only time most people heard the Bible read at all was in the public reading at worship. Thus, the readers were encouraged to put everything they had into this event, the same as a dramatic reader would in this day and time.

Remember that advertisement on television, "When E. F. Hutton speaks, people listen"? I want to tell you that when the reader stood up to proclaim the word of God from the Scriptures, believers *listened!* And it was a great honor to be selected as a reader of the Scriptures.

DISMISSALS

Godly discipline is essentially a forgotten art in the church of today. In the early church, however, such was not the case. For just prior to intercessory prayer, three groups of people, if present, were dismissed: the *seekers*, those considering the faith; the *catechumens*, those being instructed in the knowledge of the Lord, but not yet "full-fledged" members; and the *penitents*, those under discipline in the church for committing repeated acts of sin.

These were all dismissed with a blessing, not with shame. The body of Christ looked ahead to the day when these people would come to full fellowship in His church.

INTERCESSORY PRAYERS AND THE COLLECT

If you grew up in a somewhat formal church, you will no doubt remember seeing "The collect" as part of the order of worship in the church bulletin. But if you are anything like me, you had no idea what it meant. As a matter of fact, since beginning my own study of ancient worship, I have made it a point to ask other people what "the collect" is, and so far no one has been able to come up with the answer. (What is it with us human beings—we will do things over and over again and never find out *why!*)

In the early centuries of the church, when it came time for the people of God to make intercession for others and for the world, the one who presided over worship would make mention of the different petitions which had been brought for prayer. For example, he would say, "Let us now pray for the emperor." The people, on their knees, would pray either very softly or silently for that request. Then perhaps he would say, "And now let us pray for the salvation of souls in our community." Again, the people kneeling before the Lord would make this a matter of prayer. And on the intercession went until they were finished with all the petitions.

When the prayers were ended, the one in charge would stand —as would the entire congregation, often with everyone "lifting up holy hands" towards heaven—and the presbyter (elder) or bishop presiding would "collect" the prayers as he offered a final, summary prayer. The lifting up of hands signified both the position of intercession, which the priesthood of God has always assumed, and the lifting up of the collected prayers to the Lord by His earthly priesthood.

The symbolism here is magnificent. The praying church is not one where everyone prays by himself or herself and hopes that the Lord hears. True intercession is where the people of God *agree together* concerning that which is to be interceded for and *agree together* that the Lord will hear and answer. For the Scriptures teach, "If two of you agree on earth about anything that they may ask, it shall be done for them by My Father who is in heaven."[3] Thus, as one person they lift these prayers, or collect them, and present them to the Lord as an incense to Him.

Having now experienced t.is sort of intercessory prayer, it constantly amazes me how this physical involvement in prayer actually bolsters our faith as we pray. By acting out physically what is true in the spiritual or heavenly realm, we gain a new understanding of what real intercessory prayer is and the importance of standing together in agreement as we lift up those prayers that have been offered. There is power and authority here! And with the people of God agreeing together, under the authority of the church, what the will of the Lord is—think what a confidence comes in personal prayer during the week for these same petitions.

One church with which I am familiar had operated for years in what we could call, by contrast, "free-for-all" prayers. They would get together for a time of prayer, and without any real effort to sense the Lord's will, each one would pray as seemed right to him and for anything that came to mind. The matter of intercession was pretty much up for grabs.

As they began to understand the importance of the church standing together in its requests before the Lord, discerning His will, and as the people lifted their prayers as a corporate priesthood before the Lord, answered prayer became a reality. One of the elders told me recently: "We do not know of one request that we have agreed upon together as a church and lifted up together before the Lord that He has not answered!"

Did the lifting up of hands bring the answers? Of course not. God did. But by the same token, when the people began to (a) agree *together,* under the leading of the Holy Spirit and the authority of the elders, on that which should be prayed for, (b) kneel *together* as one priesthood before the Lord to offer those prayers, and (c) stand *together* with lifted hands to bring those prayers to the Lord, they learned to see by faith and action that which is true in the Spirit. The physical acts of kneeling before the Lord to pray and then standing before Him with lifted hands to collect those prayers enabled them to say with their bodies that which their minds had been trying to conceptualize for years.

The lifting up of holy hands, by the way, is not a recent phenomenon designed for use during charismatic meetings and praise gatherings. The practice goes all the way back to the Book of Exodus, where Moses lifted his hands to the Lord in intercession for Israel as it fought against the Amalekites. When Moses stood with hands lifted, Israel prevailed; when he got tired and put them down (and you *do* get tired!), Amalek prevailed.[4] Thus the official priestly stance or position of intercession was born.

The practice of lifting hands before the Lord was carried on by kings and priests throughout the Old Testament on various occasions, such as dedications of places of worship or in private prayers, as they made their requests known to God.

At the end of the Gospel of Luke, we have the record of that One who is the mediator, our High Priest pleading our cause before a holy God, ascending into heaven. In His final instructions to the disciples, He says, 'I am sending forth the promise of My Father upon you; but you are to stay in the city until you are clothed with power from on high.' And He led them out as far as Bethany, and He lifted up His hands and blessed them. And it came about that while He was blessing them, He parted from them."[5]

The last glimpse the disciples had of our Lord Jesus Christ was as He was ascending to the Father with hands lifted on high! As their mediator, soon to be crowned High King of heaven, He returned to the Father with hands lifted, interceding for those He loved and blessing them.

It is of interest that immediately following Paul's instruction that Jesus Christ is the mediator between God and man, he exhorts Timothy, "Therefore I want the men in every place to pray, lifting up holy hands, without wrath or dissension."[6] In other words, God says, "Don't come to Me divided and angry. Come with one mind, lifting up your hands as you pray."

Thus, intercessory prayer was the close of the public worship. In our picture of procession, the people of God had moved through the outer court, into the Holy Place, and were now about to enter into the Holy of Holies (into the presence of God), the way having been made open through the sacrifice of the Lord Jesus Christ.

THE KISS OF PEACE

But before the entrance into the presence of God, just before the bread and the wine were brought and the communion with the Lord begun, the *kiss of peace* was called for in the church. For we dare not enter the presence of the Lord while we are at odds with one another. Paul and Peter both make mention of such a "holy kiss" at the close of several of their letters.[7]

It is no coincidence then, that every ancient description of Christian worship makes reference to that holy kiss which came to be called the kiss of peace. Cyril of Jerusalem, writing in the fourth century, says,

> Then the Deacon cries aloud, "Receive ye one another; and let us kiss one another. Think not that this kiss ranks with those given in public with common friends. It is not such: this kiss blends souls one with another, and solicits for them entire forgiveness. Therefore this kiss is the sign that our souls are mingled together and have banished all remembrance of wrong. For this cause Christ said, 'If thou bring thy gift to the altar, and there remembereth that thy brother hath ought against thee; leave there thy gift upon the altar, and go thy way; first be reconciled to thy brother, then come and offer the gift.' The kiss therefore is reconciliation, and for this reason his Epistles urge, 'greet ye one another with a holy kiss'; and Peter, 'with a kiss of charity.'"[8]

It is one thing to be present in a crowd of several dozen or several hundred people and mentally assume that all is well before the bread and wine is consumed. It is quite another thing to look your Christian brothers and sisters in the eye and physically give them a holy embrace, *knowing* that all is well between you. And this the early church insisted upon. I cannot help but believe that much of the church today is weak because there is little assurance that the people's hearts are knitted together in love.

Hear God's warning concerning the celebrating of the Eucharist unworthily: "For this reason many among you are weak and sick, and a number sleep."[9] Many Christians suffer gross malnutrition because they never partake of the body and blood of the Lord, and therefore do not feed upon His glorified humanity. But an equal tragedy is that there is enmity and strife—or maybe just plain indifference to one another—between those who do partake. Thus, many of God's people are sick; they are infected with spiritual diseases such as biting legalism, lack of thanksgiving, lack of worship and praise, lack of true zeal. In one place, the Scriptures pinpoint such sickness as "holding to a form of godliness, although they have denied its power."[10]

I am aware that what some have called the "holy hug" is back in vogue today among many Christians. To me, that is an encouraging sign. But just the lifting up of hands can become a meaningless spiritual fad, so the embrace between brethren can erode into mere form. However, when these physical acts are accompanied by their proper spiritual exercise—that of intercessory prayer and the partaking of the Eucharist—their significance to the participants will grow and deepen.

On more than one occasion in my experience, when the church has come together to partake of the Eucharist, as the "kiss of peace" was exchanged people would actually take that moment to get things right between them. Then they would come to the table of the Lord with great joy and partake of Him with renewed confidence.

It is encouraging (and eschatologically significant) to see God restoring to His people the truths and realities of the ancient faith.

THE OFFERTORY

Today, when time for the *offertory* comes in the church service, people immediately reach for their wallets or purses. But this was not the primary thrust of the offertory in the early church.

Instead, this was the time when God's people brought forth from their own homes the bread and the wine which they had prepared for the table of the Lord. These elements represented labor and toil: the bread was made from wheat grown in the fields or purchased at the market, and the wine was made from grapes that had been grown in the courtyards of the homes. So it was a very personal and physical thing to be able to offer to the Lord and to His people the fruits of your labors which would shortly be blessed and consumed as the body and blood of Jesus Christ.

Even though we no longer live in such an agrarian culture, I find it is tremendously meaningful if, rather than the church leadership supplying the bread and wine through wholesale orders which have been delivered by truck sometime during the week, the people bring such items from their homes. This speaks so much more directly to the functioning of the body of Jesus Christ, as the people together participate in the worship of Him.

DOING WHAT WE READ

There is no end to the physical side of worship, and once the order of worship is established, there is adequate room for a variety of expression within that liturgy. For example, not long ago I was a participant in worship at a church in the Midwest. On that particular day, the theme was Psalm 150:

> Praise the Lord!
>> Praise God in His sanctuary;
>> Praise Him in His mighty expanse.
>> Praise Him for His mighty deeds;
>> Praise Him according to His excellent greatness.
>>
>> Praise Him with trumpet sound;
>> Praise Him with harp and lyre.
>> Praise Him with timbrel and dancing;
>> Praise Him with stringed instruments and pipe.
>> Praise Him with loud cymbals;
>> Praise Him with resounding cymbals.
>> Let everything that has breath praise the Lord.
>> Praise the Lord!

The unique thing about this worship experience was that the entire psalm was physically acted out by the church. And for the first time in my life, *I understood Psalm 150.* (Seeing *is* believing!)

Praise God in His sanctuary

To start things out, we gathered together outside the building where the worship service was to be held and marched in in procession. This gave us the realization that we had come together into the place where God dwells—that is, in the midst of His people. Thus the *sanctuary* was established.

Then praise was offered for His creation: for *His mighty expanse,* for *His mighty deeds,* and for *His excellent greatness,* as the psalmist says.

Praise Him with trumpet sound

At this point there was a chorus of trumpets, and an incredibly lovely interlude was offered. It was as though we were tasting of heaven itself. The musicians, by the way, were good but not excellent. The thing that *made* the worship was that the people of God had determined in their hearts to worship Him with everything at their disposal.

Praise Him with harp and lyre

And now came the stringed instruments to offer their sounds of praise to the Lord.

Praise Him with timbrel and dancing

The high point of the entire celebration of the psalm was six lovely maidens, decked out in the colored robes of the Old Testament priests who came into the room dancing together before the Lord. My heart was filled with such thanksgiving and praise that tears began to come to my eyes as I realized I was seeing a foretaste of what worship in heaven will be like. As I looked around the room, I could see that there was hardly a dry eye in our midst. In fact, those who seemed to be the more serious and staid among us were the ones who were weeping for joy the most.

Praise Him with stringed instruments and pipe

Here the guitarists and flutists gave forth their praise to God.

Praise Him with loud cymbals; Praise Him with resounding cymbals.

And at appropriate times during all of this, one brother gave tastefully intermittent crashes of the cymbals to highlight the entire affair. By the time we got to the last line of the Psalm—*Let everything that has breath praise the Lord. Praise the Lord!*—the people of God were so excited at the opportunity to offer Him worship and praise that the songs and hymns and spiritual songs that came forth were as exuberant and glorious as I have ever heard.

Now there is one thing that I must establish: This event was not some sort of emotional hype. It was the physical enactment of a passage of Scripture which most of us have heard read since we were very young. But for some reason, when we read the Psalms today, we read them only as *words*. When the Jews worshiped the Lord with the Psalms, they physically entered into that which was being read. When it says the trumpet sounded—*the trumpet sounded.* When it says they clapped their hands—*they clapped*

As believers we need to return the physical to our worship services. We have become so "mental" in our worship that it's no longer worship. It is private thought or meditation. We worship God as whole people and our wholeness includes the physical.

I believe that the church that has the courage to gain back the physical acts of worship will soon discover that their people will be alive and active in the Lord in a way they never thought possible. For the way you act at home *always* determines how you act away from home.

THE WAY THESE THINGS ARE DONE

The apostle Paul wrote to the believers in Corinth: "Let all things be done properly and in an orderly manner."[11] There was a reason for that instruction then, and there is a reason for it today.

There are some who, after reading over this chapter, will want to come out of the closet, rush into their churches, and make all of this and more happen at once! They are "fed up with the death that is there." But there is one thing worse than death: that is, a bunch of self-appointed, spiritual cheerleaders trying to get it on in worship with a group of people who swear they never will! Such worship as I am talking about here has got to be *led* by those in authority, not pulled off on the volunteer level.

To me, there is nothing more distasteful during a public worship service than having three or four people scattered throughout a room doing "something unique" to worship the Lord and embarrassing everyone else to tears. How much better to be led in worship by a godly leader who brings us as one body to the throne of God. It is so much better to *call for* the gifts of the Spirit in the church by saying, "Is there one of our number with a word for us from the Lord?" than it is for the ones with a special utterance to simply blurt it out. Such order brings far more dignity to the God we serve, and peace to His people.

As we who know the Lord seek to see the walls of worship restored in the church, let us work through and with God's appointed authorities in the order of the Spirit to produce a fruit which lasts and which tastes good in the eating.

Therefore think of the bread and wine not as merely that, for they are in fact, according to our Lord's express statement, the body and blood of Christ. For though sense suggests the mere elements, let faith assure you otherwise. Do not judge the matter from taste, but from faith be assured, without hesitation, that you have been granted the body and blood of Christ.

Cyril of Jerusalem

10

TABLE
TALK

I suppose I'll never forget the sensations I had as a child when I walked into church on Sunday morning and saw a white cloth draped over what had to be the elements of communion. As one who was not above occasionally spending his offering money for candy at the corner drugstore, and who often had his mind on things other than what was happening in church, it was not at all unusual that my immediate response was, "Oh, no—twenty minutes longer this morning!"

Communion, or what the ancients called the *Eucharist (the thanksgiving)*, never seemed to connect with anything that was going on in the rest of my life. Our church had an extremely high view of the Lord's Supper, but my honest feeling was that they couldn't deliver on the many promises they made concerning it. To me, it was purely a ritual.

And because of the way communion was presented, it was a great guilt-producing experience. Often the sermon which preceded it was little more than a spiritual spanking session. As the minister would rehearse for the people the tremendous responsibility involved in receiving the elements, and the way that all of us had consistently failed the Lord, my head dropped lower and lower and lower. Then, as if that were not enough, when he came to the place in the liturgy which talked about the one who eats and drinks unworthily being guilty of the body and the blood of the Lord,[1] I had all I could do to force myself to go up front and receive communion. So I did about the only thing a kid can do when he knows he's out of touch. I'd look around at all the others gathered there at the altar rail and think to myself, "Well, certainly I have failed the Lord and do not measure up—but he's worse," as I spotted a friend over on the other side. And I'd go ahead and partake.

Until quite recently, it has been difficult for me to admit that even after coming to faith in Christ communion has meant little or nothing to me. And I wanted it to so much. But it had been a ritual for so long that it had no meaning for me. It was difficult to shake the mental associations and attitudes I'd had in the past.

The way that the Eucharist has been forgotten by today's church does little to help strugglers like me. It seems the more zealous a church is in its preaching of personal salvation in Christ, the sloppier it is when it comes to the understanding and practice of the Lord's Supper. And when you have the feeling that the man up front conducting the service has no more understanding of what it means than you do, it does little to bolster your own faith and appreciation for that which Jesus called His body and His blood.

THE CHANGE HAS BEGUN

There are two things God used to pull me out of my "communion blues." Let me use two familiar terms to describe the process: *belief* and *practice*. In other words, coming to believe the right things about what the Eucharist is and then partaking of the body and blood of Christ in worship each Sunday has turned me completely around, to the point where I must be one of the strongest proponents for getting the Eucharist back into the worship of the church.

Let me review the biblical basis of our communion with God, and then we'll talk about what actually takes place at the table of the Lord. For unless the body and blood of Christ is a way of life for you, you will never make the connection between what it is and how it enables you to enter into the worship of God in a way that is acceptable to Him and brings assurance to you.

THE CLIMAX OF OUR PROCESSION

You will recall that in the last chapter, "The Physical Side of Worship," we introduced the idea of procession—that worship includes moving from where we have been to where we are going, into the very presence of God. We said that under the Old Testament practice, the people would march to the temple on the hill of Zion and there give praise and offer thanks to God. Likewise, there is a procession involved in our approach to God today, and we gain access to His presence through the blood of the Lamb.

In the Book of Hebrews, which so graphically portrays the work of the church as God's priesthood, we have presented to us our path or procession into the Holy of Holies. Speaking of worship under the Old Covenant, the author writes:

> The priests are continually entering the outer tabernacle, performing the divine worship, but into the second [the Holy of Holies] only the high priest enters, once a year, not without taking blood, which he offers for himself and for the sins of the people committed in ignorance. The Holy Spirit is signifying this, that the way into the holy place has not yet been disclosed, while the outer tabernacle is still standing.[2]

The point here is that in this procession the participation of the people ended *outside* the tabernacle. Only the priests were allowed inside the Holy Place, and only the high priest went further, into the Holy of Holies, and he did that just once each year. And through all of this, the Holy Spirit is saying to the people that the time for them to enter in has not yet come.

But something happened to change this on the day our Lord Jesus Christ was sacrificed on the altar of the cross. The veil of the *temple*, that which kept the people from looking into or entering the Holy of Holies, was ripped open from top to bottom.[3] Thus, the way into the very presence of God was opened.

We need to take great care here that we do not view this event as merely symbolic, or that our entrance into the presence of God is only in our minds or in our spirits. For the actual temple curtain was physically torn in two. Further, the Lord Jesus Christ rose from the dead and physically, with His resurrected body, "entered

the holy place once for all, having obtained eternal redemption."[4]
And the *place* which He physically has entered is not imaginary.

> For Christ did not enter a holy place made with hands, a mere copy
> of the true one, but into heaven itself, now to appear in the presence
> of God for us.[5]

Our Lord Jesus Christ, true God and true man in one person,
is physically present at the throne of the Father this moment as our
representative, our mediator, our intercessor, and our King! And
in our union with Him by faith through baptism, it has been
granted to us to be seated *with* Him at the right hand of the
Father.

Now let us go back and pick up on our procession to the Holy
of Holies in our worship of the Father, Son, and Holy Spirit. The
author of Hebrews goes on to say that because our Lord Jesus
Christ has entered the presence of God, we, through Him, may
enter in as well!

> Since therefore, brethren, we have confidence to enter the holy
> place by the *blood* of Jesus, by a new and living way which He
> inaugurated for us through the veil, that is, His *flesh*, and since we
> have a great high priest over the house of God, let us draw near with
> a sincere heart in full assurance of faith, having our hearts sprinkled
> clean from an evil conscience and our body washed with pure
> water.[6]

So the *terminus ad quem* of God's people is no longer outside
the gate. We are to go on in! And you see, throughout its history
the church which Christ founded has held as central to worship
that which is His body and His blood because *it was through His
body and His blood that entrance into God's presence was gained.*
He *is* the way.

And we do not come to Him alone. For we are a part of one
holy nation. And look where our procession reaches its zenith:

> But you have come to Mount Zion and the the city of the living God,
> the heavenly Jerusalem, and to myriads of angels, to the general
> assembly and church of the first-born who are enrolled in heaven,
> and to God, the judge of all, and to the spirits of righteous men
> made perfect, and to Jesus the mediator of a new covenant, and to
> the sprinkled blood. . . .[7]

Our goal in the procession of worship is to enter into the heavenly palace of God and come before His throne of glory. The object of our worship is the Father and the Son and the Holy Spirit. And present as well (as we note in the previous passage) are millions of the angelic host and the saints of God who stand in His glorious presence. To this awesome assembly of Holy God with His angelic hosts and righteous victors, what on earth could we—sinful though redeemed men—bring? Nothing but the blood of Jesus.

And so it is that the one holy church, in obedience to its Savior and King through a time-span of two thousand years, has brought to Him that once-for-all sacrifice of His body and His blood. For in the Old Covenant, one priest entered once each year with the blood of an animal. In the New Covenant, a priest*hood* enters "often" with the body and blood of Jesus Christ, as He instructed:

> And having taken some bread, when He had given thanks, He broke it, and gave it to them, saying, "This is My body which is given for you; do this in remembrance of Me." And in the same way He took the cup after they had eaten, saying, "This cup which is poured out for you is the new covenant in My blood."[8]

WHAT REALLY HAPPENS AT COMMUNION

It may well be that by now this discussion of communion is quite frustrating for you to read. If you are not regularly partaking of the body and blood of our Lord Jesus Christ in your worship experience, this will all seem rather nebulous and far-off. But it is my hope that the Word of God will motivate you to seek out the table of the Lord and call for it to be regularly celebrated where you worship. For until the church restores to centrality the praise and adoration of our Lord Jesus Christ at His table, the whole reality of worship will be unsatisfactory both for you and for God Himself. Spiritual worship indeed involves the physical.

There are several things which happen when we partake of the holy elements, and it is important for us to consider them. To exhaustively determine the benefits of this blessed mystery would be impossible, but consider with me in this brief review at least some of what occurs when we "taste and see that the Lord is good."[9]

We bring a sacrifice to God

It would be unthinkable for the priests of God to come before Him without a sacrifice. We dare not come before Him empty-handed.

"But," you protest, "our sacrifice is that one which Jesus Christ made once-for-all on the cross of Calvary. There is nothing we can add to that."

Precisely!

That is why the Lord Jesus told His followers, "This is My body which is given for you; do this in remembrance of Me." And, "This cup which is poured out for you is the new covenant in My blood."[10]

You see, the coming of the New Covenant—the new agreement which God made with man as inaugurated by the blood of Jesus—did not preclude the bringing of the physical sacrifice. Just because the blood of bulls and goats is no longer acceptable or needed does not mean there is no sacrifice at all! Indeed, our Lord Himself has made the sacrifice which we are to bring! And from the very beginning as they went about establishing His church, His apostles built this physical remembrance into the worship of the people of God, as they were commanded by Christ Himself.

Under the Old Covenant, no Jewish priest in his right mind would have dared to approach God with his hands empty. Certainly the blood of an animal was not what saved him; it was the mercy of God. Nonetheless, he was commanded to bring a sacrifice, and he did.

Where in the world, then, have we gotten the idea that under the New Covenant we come to God empty-handed? Certainly it was not bread and wine which were placed upon the cross; it was our Lord Jesus Christ whose body was broken and whose blood was shed for us. We are not saying that we are saved by bread and wine; we are saved by Him. And just as it is He who saves us, it is He who provides us—to this day—with the acceptable sacrifice.

By the way, when we say we present a sacrifice to God, we do not mean we crucify the Son of God afresh. To attempt to do so would be an abomination to the Lord. Rather we re-present the sacrifice which Jesus Christ made for our sins, as He instructed His people to do.

And when we say we bring the body and blood of Christ, we do not pretend to know how that is so, any more than we can explain how one is born anew, or how Christ calmed the sea or came back from the dead. We do, nonetheless, confess without compromise that these things are true. When it came to explaining *how* it was that the elements of the Eucharist were the body and blood of Christ, the ancients could only proclaim, "O blessed mystery!" Not until the scholasticism of the twelfth and thirteenth centuries, when people tried to bring such things under the scrutiny of human rationalism, were attempts made to label the mystery *transubstantiation*, and then much later *consubstantiation*.

In our day, we need to bring human reason back under the law of faith where it belongs and gain back a holistic view of God's power and His sacred mysteries. It is not for us to know *how* the bread and wine is the body and blood of Christ, for "So are My ways higher than your ways," declares the Lord.[11] We need not concern ourselves with chemical change; it is not "better living through chemistry"! Instead, we must talk of God's power and mysteries.

We partake of His life

Now let's get something straight here. We evangelicals preach with zeal a passage from the third chapter of the Gospel of John where our Lord Jesus Christ teaches, "*Unless* one is born again, he cannot see the kingdom of God."[12] We rightly tell the world: "No new birth—no eternal life."

But do you realize that that exact word, "unless," is used again in John 6? Jesus said, "*Unless* you eat the flesh of the Son of Man and drink His blood, you have no life in yourselves."[13]

Why is it that so many Christians are willing to fight to the death for "unless one is born again, he cannot see the kingdom of God" and at the same time absolutely ignore the "unless" of John 6, having to do with the body and blood of Jesus Christ as that which gives us life in the Eucharist? People, let us return to the biblical faith!

We do not receive spiritual food by mental assent, any more than we witness for Christ by sitting home *thinking* about the lost, or feed the hungry by *willing* it to be so! There is a physical side to being spiritual! We cannot get around that point in Scripture. Jesus said, "For My flesh is true food, and My blood is true drink."[14] And pastors who have denied their people the body and blood of Jesus Christ at regular intervals of worship, and theologians who have explained it all away, are robbing Christ's sheep of lifegiving nourishment. They will be called upon for an answer.

"But," you may protest, "it is through the Holy Spirit that we receive life." Of course it is. It was Jesus Himself who said, "It is the Spirit who gives life; the flesh profits nothing; the words that I have spoken to you are spirit and are life."[15] Eating the flesh of Christ is without profit unless the Holy Spirit gives life in that eating. This is why the Christian church adopted the *epiclesis*, a specific invitation for the heavenly Father to send His Spirit upon the elements, that they indeed would be the body and blood of Christ and, as such, bring nourishment to the faithful.

Thus, we confess that the Holy Spirit does give us life through the very flesh of Christ. Otherwise, if the body and blood of Christ were not necessary for our life, why would the eternal Son of God have become incarnate? For it is, after all, the incarnate Christ who is the mediator between God and man, *not* the Holy Spirit. As we partake of the body and blood of the Son of God, however, *the Spirit of God has a means through which to give us His life*. For God, as we have noted, has from the very beginning transmitted that which is spiritual through that which is physical.

We commune with the saints

Do you realize that the table of the Lord is not simply composed of those who gather around it in a local church situation? The table of the Lord is twenty centuries long! And, if our understanding of Hebrews 11 includes an unbroken lineage of the people of God throughout Old Testament history (I believe it does!), then those same ones who surround us as our great cloud of witnesses also commune with us in heavenly places. At the head of the table, of course, is our King of Kings, our Lord Jesus Christ, the Father, and the Holy Spirit. Add to this all of the saints of the ages and the angelic hosts, and you have quite a gathering! This is why in the hymn "The Church's One Foundation" we have that glorious line, "And mystic sweet communion with those whose rest is won."

The Eucharist has incredible eschatological or future implications. As we gather around the table of the Lord in this dispensation, we are a part of a coming kingdom which will one day be fully revealed. For though our Lord Jesus is our servant or our host at this table today, that great day is coming when He will partake with us in His eternal kingdom at the marriage feast of the Lamb.

We enter the Holy of Holies

As we have noted earlier, in the Old Testament only the high priest was allowed inside the Holy of Holies one day each year as he brought with him that blood sacrifice. But in the New Covenant, all who are part of the new Israel, the church, have become a corporate priesthood unto God. That is why the writer of Hebrews says;

> But you have come to Mount Zion [Jerusalem] and to the city of the living God, the heavenly Jerusalem, and to myriads of angels, to the general assembly and church of the first-born who are enrolled in heaven, and to God, the judge of all, and to the spirits of righteousness men made perfect, [That's the communion of the saints!], and to Jesus, the mediator of a new covenant, and to the sprinkled blood. . . .[16]

Do you realize the sphere of your worship? You see, as we bring to the Lord that one sacrifice which is acceptable, the body and blood of Jesus Christ, through the Holy Spirit we enter *God's very presence!* We come with confidence to the heavenly place of God's dwelling, the very Holy of Holies, and we bring our thanksgiving and praise to Him *there.* It is Christ's sacrifice—which we now bring again—that has made us acceptable before God.

I wonder if it is not because we have ignored the worship of Christ at the Eucharist that Christians today have tended to an unhealthy mysticism. Not a few times have I heard someone say, "I turned to my spirit to praise the Lord." We do not turn inside, but to God Himself. The reason Christ lives in our hearts is to enable us to commune with the Lord in heavenly places, *not* to turn inside ourselves to worship.

Our Lord Jesus prayed "lifting up His eyes to heaven."[17] We, too, come to the heavenly city, to the throne of God on high. And what a thrill it is for a church which worships the Lord at His table to have this full realization of exactly *where they are entering* when they bring their offerings to Him!

We remember our forgiveness and deliverance

We have considered already our Lord's instruction to partake of the bread and the cup *in remembrance of* Him. To gain a better insight into what that means, let us consider the ancient Jewish Feast of Passover. In the centuries following their deliverance from Pharaoh, godly Jews feasted annually in remembrance of their release from captivity. But it was more than a mental observance. Those at the feast were instructed, in the celebration, to view themselves as having been *personally delivered* from the hands of the enemy.

And so it is at the feast of the Holy Eucharist. It goes beyond a show-and-tell time to teach us a Bible history lesson. As we eat His flesh and drink His blood, we receive into ourselves a personal forgiveness. That cup is His blood in the New Covenant. That blood forever washes *me*. *My* sins are forever covered through His blood shed for *me*. *My* guilt is forever banished through the blood of Christ sprinkled for *me* on heaven's mercy seat. *My* sins have been separated from *me* as far as the east is from the west.[18]

For the Christian, remembrance is far more than mentally walking backwards to the cross. It is partaking of Christ's very sacrifice today, knowing that every sin he ever has committed or ever will commit was nailed to the cross of Jesus Christ and forgiven through His atonement.

We confess we are one in Christ

The apostle Paul wrote, "Is not the bread which we break a sharing in the body of Christ? Since there is one bread, we who are many are one body; for we all partake of the one bread."[19]

Clearly, if we wish to declare our identity with the church of

Jesus Christ, this is accomplished by partaking of the bread of the Eucharist. Occasionally you will hear a statement like, "I just want to be one with the Lord's people wherever they may be. So I have not tied myself down to a church. That way, there is no barrier to simple fellowship in Jesus."

In my opinion, it is in large part because the Protestant church has neglected the Eucharist that its people no longer have a biblical view of the church. When the bread is hidden from view, the body of Christ, the church, becomes invisible as well. For without the physical manifestation of the loaf, the spiritual reality of the body of Christ will cease to be present.

On the other hand, as the people of God become awakened to Christ again by the Holy Spirit, they begin to talk almost immediately of one thing (and this has happened repeatedly in history): the church. As you partake of the one loaf in the Eucharist, you are confessing that you are sharing in the body of Christ with all others who do the same. When the people of God begin once again to share the meal His Son instituted, the prospects of the fractured church finding its oneness again in His body will be less and less remote.

We proclaim the Lord's death until He comes

In order for communication to take place, words are not necessarily needed. Often what one does is more important than what one says. If you desire to be fully evangelical, to be a person who bears a complete witness to the whole gospel, then take your place regularly at the table of the Lord. For it is there, "you proclaim the Lord's death until He comes."[20] There are no sermons, Scripture memory plans, printed literature, or New Testament distribution agencies which can ever take the place of the Eucharist in this facet of Christian witness. The deposit of the truth of the substitutionary death of the Lord Jesus Christ for the sins of the world is there at His table. Apart from it, according to the Scriptures, we will never know the full reality of the proclamation of His death.

GOD WANTS AN ANSWER

We are at a crossroads in our culture. It is as though God is forcing His people to take sides on so many issues. For example, are we going to stand on the sexual morality of the historic church, or will we go with the modern belief in free love and homosexuality as a valid alternative? Will we hold to the sanctity of life to which our fathers held, or will we side with the wholesale abortionists? Will we submit to the Holy Scriptures as the inspired, authoritative revelation of God to His church, or will we follow the higher critics?

And will we return to the table of the Lord to partake of His body and His blood and take our stand with the one holy church? Or will we stay with the undernourished and the invisible, peering into the life of His kingdom from the outside?

I can do all things through Him [Christ] who strengthens me.

Paul to the Philippians

11

WORKING TOGETHER

Since there is a physical side to being spiritual, since things like the human body are precious in God's sight, then certainly bringing the total person under the reign of Christ is paramount. Yet Christians struggle with just *how* to get in gear to do God's will. That is, how do we orchestrate all that we are—our bodies, our minds, our feelings and emotions, our human spirits—to submit harmoniously to actually *do* what we know to be the will of God?

Saint Francis of Assisi writes about "Brother Ass," his nickname for his own body, and how difficult it was for him to bring that stubborn critter under the control of the Holy Spirit. In his *Confessions,* Saint Augustine makes it very clear that it was God who made him in his flesh and how marvelous that creation was. At one point, when he speaks of the habitual sins which had become a part of him, he says, "For I have gone over all the evidence of my flesh, but cannot find by which they (my sins) enter."[1]

Centuries earlier, the apostle Paul said of his struggles with godliness, "I see a different law in the members of my body, waging war against the law of my mind, and making me a prisoner of the law of sin which is in my members."[2]

We moderns express these things in somewhat different

143

terms, yet the warfare of bringing ourselves in obedience under the lordship of Jesus Christ and the power of His Holy Spirit continues. It occurs to us quite early in our lives that we are not by nature obedient people and that our "human" response is to let our fallenness get the best of us.

We have discussed coming to the Lord by faith and in baptism being brought to a vital union with Christ through the power of the Holy Spirit. Then we reviewed how we are regularly nourished by the body and blood of our Lord Jesus, partaking in the Encharist of His resurrected humanity. Now, we come to that matter of walking daily in the Spirit as physical people in a material world.

THE "TUBE" SOLUTION

In contemporary Christian circles, the solution to this dilemma of how to be holy is usually, "God will do it through us. Jesus Christ will live *His* life through *ours.* Since we are incapable of doing anything to please God, the Holy Spirit will take such complete charge that it is no longer we who live for God, but He who lives through us."

It was this "tube theology" that I was taught shortly after giving my life to Christ. The thing about it that helped me most was that it enabled me to take my trust in myself as my determinative leader and transfer it to the Lord. And sure enough, I found out that He did supply me with the power to live a new life. There was no difficulty here at all.

The problem was with the long-term implications, and ultimately my concepts. If we believe that we have a God who does *everything* through us and that we are incapable of doing *anything* ourselves, eventually that is how we will behave.

The frustrating thing was that I would go back and read through the Scriptures, trying to find some biblical support for this theology. But it wasn't there! I knew in my heart that "God will do everything through you" was an overstatement, yet I couldn't put my finger on what the proper statement was.

For me, the long-term fruit of tube theology was a passive Christianity. For if we *literally* believe God will do everything through us, we take little or no initiative to do anything. Taken out to its logical extreme, tube theology becomes a dehumanizing belief; people are nothing, and thus we go too far in discrediting the physical or human portion of God's creation.

Part of the reason for the underemphasis on the role of a redeemed human being in carrying out God's will would appear to be centered in our view of ourselves, specifically of our bodies. We talk about our "sinful selves" and tend to make ourselves synonymous with sin. And therein lies the problem.

Your *body* is not evil. The father of evil is the devil, and he works through the powers of sin and death. Thus, you are not your enemy. Your body is not your foe. If you yield your body to unrighteousness, then it becomes the vehicle through which sin is expressed; if you yield your body to righteousness, it becomes the instrument for doing good. This is Paul's whole argument in Romans 6:12, 13, where he writes,

> Therefore do not let sin reign in your mortal body that you should obey its lusts, and do not go on presenting the members of your body to sin as instruments of unrighteousness; but present yourselves to God as those alive from the dead, and your members as instruments of righteousness to God.

So your enemy here is the power of sin. It is not your body, not your soul or mind, not you. Understand this: When you come to Christ and submit yourself to His righteousness, you and your body are His property to be used by Him. Do not call His possession your foe! That sort of thing produces self-hatred and ultimately hatred for God as your Creator. Your body is not evil. It is wonderfully formed in God's image, and bought back for His use through the blood of Jesus Christ. Yield it to Him for His glory and active use.

THE "BOOTSTRAP" SOLUTION

But what seemed to me to be the only alternative to tube theology was the plan where *we* end up doing everything. Call it "bootstrap theology." And that seemed far worse. As a matter of fact, it was this basic philosophy out of which I had been rescued when I committed my life to Christ.

Bootstrap theology is just another name for justification by works. Under this program, if you have a view of God at all, you view Him as essentially having given you all the brains you need, so now get out there and *do it*. Bootstrappers give the rest of us a fit about not using our own "natural resources" to live the Christian life. But what they forget is that our natural resources were seriously depleted through sin, and thus we need *super*natural resources to make it once again.

There was never any real temptation to go back to being a bootstrapper. And I was afraid to let go of being a tuber. Because that was what my crowd of Christians taught. They certainly had their set of Bible verses to back them up. But what troubled me was that *other set* of verses which seemed to teach some sort of human response or perseverance or integrity, but which never seemed to be preached in tube-theology churches.

As the years went by, having not resolved the dilemma in my own mind, I simply quit trying to define how it is that God works in us. I still believed, practiced, and taught the full work of the Holy Spirit, but when it came right down to "where the rubber meets the road," as to exactly what *He* did and exactly what *I* did, I was hard-pressed to give an answer.

THE GREEKS HAVE A WORD FOR IT: *SYNERGISM*

Then one day in a conversation with some fellow-Christians, someone dropped the word "synergism" on me. It was one of those situations where there were just enough people around to make it uncomfortable for me to ask, "What does that mean?" So I simply kept quiet. Little more was said about the word at that point, other than that it was such a helpful concept to the man who had used the word because it had helped him to a new conceptualizing of the Christian life. I went home and got out the books!

Paul wrote, "For we are God's fellow-workers."[3] In the Greek the word "fellow-workers" is *synergoi*, from which we get our English derivative *synergism* or *synergy*. The prefix *syn* means "the same as" (synonymous) or "together with" (synthesis), and the *ergy* from *ergos* means "work" or "energy." Thus, synergism is a word to describe "working along with" or "working together with."

You see, God is not after tubes, but people. By the new birth,

He did not make us slaves, but sons. (And sons who, by the way, willingly submit to Him as His slaves or workers.)

WHAT SYNERGISM ISN'T

Before we look into the Scriptures to discover just how we work along with God, let me first begin by describing what synergism is not. For in the past, the term has been suspect by those who were afraid it inferred some things contrary to faith.

It's not earning merit with God. If I say that my son earns favor with me because he cooperates with me by mowing the lawn, I would be missing the whole point of a father-son relationship. As my son, he *has* my favor and my love. Because we are related in that way, I expect him to do what I say. And though he pleases me with his actions, he could mow one million lawns and I could not love him any more.

So when we say that man participates with the Lord or cooperates with Him, we do not mean that man gains points with God by doing so. Rather, we say along with James, "You show me a man's faith, and I'll show you his works."[4] What we do, our fruit, becomes the evidence of our union with Christ, not the means to it.

Synergism is not "God is my co-pilot." Under that precarious system, I'm in the left-hand seat as pilot, with the Lord over on the right-hand side as my back-up. And that's not even close! In being fellow-workers with God, we do not mean the teaming up of two equals.

Rather, by *synergism* we mean that the actual living out of our union with Jesus Christ *as Lord* requires the cooperation of two unequal but equally necessary persons: Christ and me.

SOME INCREDIBLE EXAMPLES

Think back through the Scriptures for a moment and see if you can name at least a dozen instances—from memory alone—where God spoke and people carried out His will, and where without such cooperation the will of God would not have been done.

Let's take, for example, the incident at the Red Sea. Who parted the sea? God. Who marched through? Moses and the people of Israel. Did God march through the Red Sea for them? Absolutely not. He made the way, and they walked through.

Or Noah and the ark. Who told Noah to build the ark? God did. Who built it? Noah. According to specifications? You bet. Did he get those from God? Absolutely. Did God create the trees out of which the ark was made? No question about it. God gave the orders and provided Noah with the materials, but it was Noah who did the work and put the boat together.

When the whole thing was made, who provided the water, God or Noah? But once the rains came, who sailed the waters?

Perhaps the greatest all-time illustration of synergism would be our blessed Mary. Through whom was Jesus conceived? The Holy Spirit. In whose womb? Mary's. By whose will? The Father's. But who carried our Lord for His nine-month period of gestation? It was Mary. Who arranged the songs in the heavens at His birth? God did. But at whose breasts did the Lord Jesus feed? Mary's.

Now, what two parties were *absolutely necessary* for the whole drama of the virgin birth to have occurred? The bootstrapper may say, "It was no virgin birth at all. A young woman simply gave birth to another human being." Or the super-saint, tube-theologian may say, "Well, we know that God really did it." But it takes little imagination to see how the Lord God overshadowed a completely human woman, and within her womb was conceived One who was fully of His nature—divine—and of her nature— human—our Lord and Savior Jesus Christ.

THE BIBLE SAYS . . .

Thus, as you go back through the Scriptures with the perspective of synergism, suddenly it becomes as plain as day. Those verses which only seem to teach that God does it all, in context, come through with the human element as well. And those passages which, out of context, seem to say that it's man who gets the job done are brought back into focus under the lordship of Jesus Christ.

Perhaps the classic passage in all the New Testament on how man cooperates with God to do His will is:

So then, my beloved, just as you have always obeyed, not as in my

presence only, but now much more in my absence, work out your
salvation with fear and trembling; for it is God who is at work in you,
both to will and to work for His good pleasure.[5]

If you go to a bootstrap church, the message will be, "Work
out your own salvation." I have heard many such sermons in my
lifetime. And there's no need to explain how frustrating this challenge is. Categorically, it is impossible to accomplish this exhortation without the rest of the passage.

On the other hand, I don't know how many messages I've
heard from tube theologians on "God at work within you" in which
believers are encouraged to "let Jesus do it all." And then those
same preachers wonder why they can't get their people to do
much!

(In fact, someone was saying just the other day how remarkable it is in Roman Catholic churches: it always seems that the
people are busy with volunteer work, church functions, and in
general are there on time, getting things done. But in evangelical
churches it's like pulling teeth to get the people to really pitch in
and work. Do you care to take a wild guess as to why this might be
true?)

When you go back to Philippians 2 and read what Paul had to
say, in context, suddenly the whole thing makes sense. The salvation he's talking about there is the daily deliverance that God gives
to His people. And the overall subject is obedience to Christ under
Paul's apostolic authority. Let us be quick to agree with the apostle
that if we're going to be delivered daily from the power of evil and
be saved from its control, we'd better not sit around and wait for
Jesus to do it all through us. Because it just so happens that Jesus
Christ has given us the power through our union and communion
with Him to say no to degradation, and to do so with fear and
trembling.

But on the other hand, as we say no to sin and start to build a
repertoire of righteousness, let's not get caught reading our own
press clippings! For if we forget that it is God who works within us,
deciding both what we are to do and energizing us to do it, we'll fall
right back into our old do-it-yourself living.

My heart sings with praise at the clarity of the Scriptures on this issue. I cannot express how grateful I am to have begun to lay hold of the concept of spirituality which has been taught by our Lord Jesus Christ, by His apostles, and which has been practiced by the church.

Or take another familiar passage of Scripture, also out of Paul's letter to the Philippians: "I can do all things through Him who strengthens me."[6] How much clearer can you get? In this passage, who is it that does all things? Well, contrary to the tubers, it is *you!* But where on earth do you get the strength to do it? Nowhere on earth. For it is *only* through the strength of Jesus Christ that you can carry out the will of God.

Do you see how clear this cooperation is? God gives you the orders, gives you the power, and you as His cooperative worker (not equal with Him, but in union with His Son) carry out His will in your physical body.

Or what about that great verse that most of us in the evangelical tradition have used for years in our invitations for Christian commitment? "Behold, I stand at the door and knock; if any one hears My voice and opens the door, I will come in to him, and will dine with him, and he with Me."[7] Talk about synergism! The one standing at the door waiting to provide that lovely communion and friendship is our Lord Jesus Christ. But we are the ones who have freedom to open the door or leave it closed. He knocks, He gives life, and it is we who answer His call.

You say, "How does all this fit into the doctrine of predestination?" Absolutely perfectly, if you recall that the Scriptures also teach the freedom of choice for the human race. Certainly God knows ahead of time who will do what; if He did not, He would no longer be omniscient God. But we also believe that in His sovereignty He created people to exercise their freedom to choose Him or reject Him.

ILLUSTRATIONS ARE SO IMPORTANT

One of the reasons we have gotten ourselves into trouble and have strayed from orthodox doctrine (be it concerning spirituality, the church, good works, or whatever) is that we have manufactured our own modern illustrations to explain spiritual truth at the expense of using the ones set down for us in Scripture. This is not to say we must use only biblical illustrations; it is to say that the illustrations we use had better be biblical!

Take the matter of living the Christian life. I've heard illustrations to explain how God works in us ranging from "the hand in the glove" (Jesus is the hand; we are the glove), to "water through a pipe" (the Holy Spirit is the water; we are the pipe), to "the hub, the spokes, and the wheel" (God is the hub; our actions are the spokes, and the wheel is the balanced life which results), and many more which attempt to describe the Christian life.

While we certainly may find some elements of truth in these illustrations, the pictures of spirituality in Scripture are infinitely more accurate. Take the one our Lord Jesus Christ Himself used as recorded in John 15: the vine and the branches. Jesus said:

> I am the true vine, and My Father is the vinedresser. Every branch in Me that does not bear fruit, He takes away; and every branch that bears fruit, He prunes it, that it may bear more fruit. You are already clean because of the word which I have spoken to you. Abide in Me, and I in you. As the branch cannot bear fruit of itself, unless it abides in the vine, so neither can you, unless you abide in Me. I am the vine, you are the branches; he who abides in Me, and I in him, he bears much fruit; for apart from Me you can do nothing.[8]

Now stack that passage up against the hand in the glove. Notice that all the objects in the above passage are animate—they are *alive*. God the Father, who is the gardener, is certainly active. The Son of God, Jesus Christ, who is the vine, is alive. Even the branches (that's us) are alive, though we see in this illustration that their (our) life is derived from the vine, Jesus Christ.

The hand in the glove metaphor is not only inaccurate, but if taken literally will lead its adherents astray. For though the hand is alive, the glove is not, and it never can be. It is only a passive piece of leather which actually serves to conceal the hand. Furthermore, whereas the branches are in vital living union with the vine, the glove can never become joined with the hand. At best, it is alienation with proximity. And the other illustrations fall equally short.

How often in the Scripture has God been pictured as the Father and the believer as a son? Again, a *living relationship*. Or

what about the shepherd and the sheep? What a beautiful, inti-
mate, living picture of the guidance of Jesus Christ over our lives.

I'm not saying we should never use illustrations from contemporary daily life. My only plea is that we be sure they are conform-
able to the Scriptures and do not end up putting the people of God
under a sense of worthlessness or passivity.

THE PHYSICAL AND THE SPIRITUAL

To tie it all together—we simply can't be spiritual without
being physical. For man was never created to be either *just* a soul
or *just* a body. We are not one or the other, but *both*. And until
we, as believers are in synergy with Christ and all that He is, we
will be frustrated in trying to live under His reign.

The fact is, God does not do it all through us; He works within
us that we might do His will. Without Him we can do nothing. But
please don't stop there. For the Scripture says we can do all things
through Christ who strengthens us. Both statements are true and
must be taken together.

Remember: your body has been washed with pure water. You
have been united with Christ by baptism and have been made a
new creation. You are to partake of the body and blood of Christ to
be fully nourished and strengthened by His glorified human nature. And God wants to take you—all that you are—and direct you
by His Holy Spirit to do His will. He wants to use your body, your
brain, your spirit, and whatever else goes into making up the total
person that you are.

He does not want you sitting idly by, wondering when He will
next do something through you. Nor does He want you out hus-
tling up His business on your own, striving to do His will. Instead,
learn to live out your union with Him, living under His reign in the
church, thereby knowing His will and doing what He says to do.

And those from among you will rebuild the ancient ruins; you will raise up the age-old foundations; and you will be called the repairer of the breach, the restorer of the streets in which to dwell.

Isaiah

12

AN

ERA OF RECONSTRUCTION

What better place to end a treatise on the physical side of being spiritual than to look ahead to the physical return of our Lord Jesus Christ for His bride, the church, and our preparation for that great event?

We have considered the glory it is for us to have been created human beings and to bear the image of God in His creation. We saw, as well, the amazing order of His world and how this, too, speaks of His character. We dealt with our estrangement from God because of our sins, and how we have physically acted out our sinfulness.

Then, in leading up to the drama of our redemption in Jesus Christ, we considered the countless ways in which God manifested Himself to us through physical phenomena, how He so carefully chose the beloved Virgin Mary to be the bearer of His Son, and why our Lord Jesus Christ had to become fully man in order to save us.

Next, we turned to the physical ways in which we relate to God. We said that being a Christian is not a matter of every person reporting in before God alone and by self-appointment, but that He has established a nation, a church—visible and locatable—in which He might be known and served. The entrance He provided into His kingdom is through the water and the Spirit; there is a physical side to being born again. Our worship of Him carries with it the idea of procession, beginning as we turn our minds and hearts to Him through singing and the reading of the Scriptures, then physically lifting up our prayers in the Spirit to Him, bringing Him the fruits of our labors, and—the climax of it all—partaking of the body and blood of our Lord Jesus Christ. Then we talked about how the priesthood of God lives out its union with Him in the world: how we behave. But what about the promises which await us?

THE SPIRIT AND THE BRIDE

Now and again we hear the question posed, "What sort of bride is Jesus Christ coming back to claim?" And with great care not to attach some man-made label or denominational designation to the answer, the reply is more often than not, "Oh, He will return for a *spiritual* bride."

But think about that for a moment! On the purely human level, what sort of man would want to enter into the matrimonial bond with only that which is spiritual! Even the most staunch and dedicated sixteenth-century pietist would hold out for more than that.

I'll never forget a late-evening discussion with some of my classmates in the dorm at seminary back in 1961. Each man was trying to describe the mental picture he had of the girl he wished he could marry. Naturally, the conversation began on a very sanctimonious and pristine level, and then steadily came down to the realities of earthly living. The man who received consensus honors as stating his own preferences in the most honest and forthright manner was the one who said, "Really, guys, if we told it as it is, what we're all after is a spiritual Marilyn Monroe."

And when you consider God's description of the bride of Jesus Christ in the Scriptures, you discover that it is not just a spiritual bride He is coming back to claim. The bride He is awaiting is physical as well. In a word, she is *both*. In fact, take note of the brilliant synergism of the spiritual and the physical as you read John's description of the eternal bride of Christ:

And he carried me away in the Spirit to a great and high mountain, and showed me the holy city, Jerusalem, coming down out of heaven from God, having the glory of God. Her brilliance was like a very costly stone, as a stone of crystal-clear jasper.

It had a great and high wall, with twelve gates, and at the gates twelve angels; and names were written on them, which are those of the twelve tribes of the sons of Israel.

There were three gates on the east and three gates on the north and three gates on the south and three gates on the west.

And the wall of the city had twelve foundation stones, and on them were the twelve names of the twelve apostles of the Lamb.

And the one who spoke with me had a gold measuring rod to measure the city, and its gates and its wall.

And the city is laid out as a square, and its length is as great as the width; and he measured the city with the rod, fifteen hundred miles; its length and width and height are equal.

And he measured its wall, seventy-two yards, according to human measurements, which are also angelic measurements.

And the material of the wall was jasper; and the city was pure gold, like clear glass.

The foundation stones of the city wall were adorned with every kind of precious stone.[1]

Here we have such things as *walls, gates, foundation stones, gold,* and *precious building stones.* Suddenly, a host of other Scriptures come back to mind.

—Jesus said to Peter, "Upon this *rock* I will build My church."[2]

—And He told the Twelve, "In My Father's house are many *dwelling places* . . . I go to prepare a place for you."[3]

—And Peter writes to us, "You also, as *living stones,* are being built up as a spiritual *house* for a holy priesthood."[4]

—And Paul encouraged the Ephesians, "*You* are fellow-citizens with the saints, and are of God's *household,* having been built upon the *foundation* of the apostles and the prophets, Christ Jesus Himself being the *corner stone,* in whom the whole *building,* being fitted together is growing into a holy *temple* in the Lord."[5]

—And again, "We are to grow up in all aspects into Him, who is the head, even Christ, from whom the whole body, being *fitted and held together* by that which every joint supplies, according to the proper working of *each individual part.*"[6]

There's no question at all about what is in view here. We are those objects! But this is certainly not a splattering of isolated Christians all across the earth who have no vital or ordered connection with one another. No, what is being described here is the church, the people of God as a *structure*, a *family*, a grouping of human *physical components* being put together as a dwelling place for God. It is the physical and the spiritual in majestic concert.

People motivated by the promised coming of the Lord have done some interesting things throughout history. Some have exhibited strange reactions, such as heading for the mountains dressed in bed linens, picking dates for His return, or setting up curious political-prophetic game plans for the future.

But in the Scriptures the exhortations surrounding the promise of Christ's return consistently have to do with shoring things up in the household of God and in the lives of His people. In fact, was not the entire Book of Revelation addressed from "John to the seven *churches* that are in Asia,"[7] challenging them to repent and clean house in the light of the second coming of Jesus Christ?

A FORMER RESTORATION

The church of Jesus Christ is in sore need of restoration today. She is in great disrepair. The priesthood is too often without godly authority and direction, the walls of worship have been torn down, and the poor have been neglected while we have looked after ourselves. As a result, we who should be full have become famished *and do not even know it!*

Turn with me to a time in history when many of the conditions in the midst of God's people were remarkably similar. The writer of the account we will read is the prophet Haggai, and his job was the rebuilding of the temple in about 520 B.C. The people were claiming that it was not yet time for them to roll up their sleeves and put their bodies to work in the reconstruction project, but the Lord had a different view!

> "Thus says the Lord of hosts, 'This people says, "The time has not come, even the time for the house of the Lord to be rebuilt."'"
> Then the word of the Lord came by Haggai the prophet saying, "Is it time for you yourselves to dwell in your paneled houses while this house lies desolate?"

Now therefore, thus says the Lord of hosts, "Consider your ways! You have sown much, but harvest little; you eat, but there is not enough to be satisfied; you drink, but there is not enough to become drunk; you put on clothing, but no one is warm enough; and he who earns, earns wages to put into a purse with holes."[8]

The people of God had been living in high style. Their homes were built and decorated in such a way that had there been a *Town and Country* magazine in that day and time, most likely some of them would have been featured. But the house of God was in ruins, an embarrassment to all.

And do you see the lesson here? When believers look after themselves first, neglecting one another and the worship and reign of the Lord, *everything* is affected. Here were food-producers starving, fully clothed people freezing to death. They not only had holes in their pockets where their money dropped through, but they were unable even to get buzzed from what they drank.

Until we, God's people today, turn from our individualism and our arm's-length attitudes toward sharing, giving, coming under the authority of the church, entering into godly worship and thanksgiving, and the rest of what His kingdom offers, *we will not be satisfied.* Here we are, running from one Christian seminar to the next, one speaker to the next, one study group to the next, one evangelism plan to the next, one new spiritual theme or fad to the next, and still we're coming up cold, bored, and hungry. It is a kind of escapism, and it has even the pastors on the run. And all the time God is saying, "Why not get off your merry-go-round and help Me restore My temple?"

Or, to quote Him precisely,

"Go up to the mountains, bring wood and rebuild the temple, that I may be pleased with it and be glorified," says the Lord.

"You look for much, but behold, it comes to little; when you bring it home, I blow it away. Why?" declares the Lord of hosts, "Because of My house which lies desolate, while each of you runs to his own house.

"Therefore, because of you the sky has withheld its dew, and the earth has withheld its produce."[9]

THE TASK AT HAND

I say, with all the conviction of my heart, this is God's Word for you and me today. Before the Lord Jesus Christ returns, the will of the Father is for the bride to be in glorious order—physically and spiritually—as the eternal dwelling place of God among men. And we have to see that, by the power of the Holy Spirit, we are to be making ourselves ready now. God has never promised us that He'd wave a magic wand and get His house in order at the instant of His Son's return. No, like the virgins of old, we are to have our lamps full of oil and trimmed.

And do not bank on just a "spiritual" relationship with a God who is also constructing a *city*. Be found present there as well! Renovation and adornment are the program now, in advance of His coming. Then, for those who are in union with Him, feasting in His halls, unashamed of being bride or martyr, the day of the Lord will come gloriously.

It seems that just as soon as you become enamored of being a peacemaker, God has to remind you once again that His peacemaker also wears a sword. It is time to come back home to Mother! What better hour than now for the people of God to get back to the faith of the one holy church? Take your stand in a church that believes and practices the historic orthodox Christian faith, its sacraments and its life. Put your time and effort in *there*.

If you are impressed with some of the creative ways that extra-church groups are trying to reach out, use these ideas under the authority and care of the church. In so doing, the people you reach will be born to a family, not an agency. Call for your friends in religious speciality movements to submit themselves and their programs to the government of God in the church.

Learn to call for *continued* progress in regaining such things as baptism and communion. The Holy Spirit has been doing some encouraging things among the people of God. So don't be content with old victories. Continue to be used of Him to rebuild the church upon its once-laid, ancient foundations. For the day of the Lord is at hand.

We've had our fling. We've danced on the fringes of pop religion and have continued to hunger and thirst. We've marched to the beat of our modern drummers. Let us now take the enthusiasm which the Spirit of God has breathed back into His people and bring it to the center of the faith, that the fruit might remain.

And the people be preserved—both physically and spiritually.

NOTES

Chapter 1

1. 1 Corinthians 12:21.
2. Donald E. Hoke, ed., *Evangelicals Face the Future* (South Pasadena, California: William Carey Library, 1978), p. 116.
3. Jacques Ellul, *The Presence of the Kingdom* (New York: The Seabury Press, 1967), p. 14.
4. Romans 6:12.

Chapter 2

1. John 4:24.
2. 1 John 5:12.
3. From the pre-publication transcript of Metropolitan Anthony Bloom's address to Lambeth XI, Summer, 1978. The book *Discerning God's Will*, by James Simpson and Edward Story, recording the Lambeth Conference, will be published in 1979 by Thomas Nelson Publishers.
4. Genesis 1:1,2.
5. Romans 1:20,21.
6. Colossians 1:16.
7. Genesis 1:2.
8. Genesis 1:26.
9. Genesis 1:31.
10. Psalm 100:3.
11. Ephesians 5:29.
12. 1 Corinthians 7:4.
13. Psalm 19:1.
14. Romans 1:21,22.

15. Henry Bettenson, ed., *The Early Christian Fathers* (London: Oxford University Press, 1956), p. 103.

Chapter 3

1. Romans 12:1.
2. Romans 12:2.
3. Romans 10:9.
4. James 4:8.
5. James 3:8,9.
6. Revelation 2:7.
7. Galatians 4:26.
8. Revelation 21:9.
9. Genesis 1:26-31.
10. Isaiah 40:28.
11. Leviticus 19:2, and numerous other passages.
12. Henry Bettneson, ed. and tr., *The Later Christian Fathers* (London: Oxford University Press, 1970), p. 130.
13. John 17:3.
14. Genesis 3:24.
15. Athanasius, *On the Incarnation,* (Crestwood: St. Vladimir's Seminary Press, 1944), p. 28.
16. Romans 1:21.
17. Genesis 18:25.
18. Matthew 15:8.
19. 1 Peter 1:16.
20. Romans 6:11.
21. 2 Peter 1:4.
22. 2 Timothy 2:21.
23. Romans 5:20.
24. 1 Corinthians 6:20.

Chapter 4

1. Hebrews 1:1,2.
2. Genesis 5:24; Hebrews 11:5.
3. Acts 8:39,40.
4. Hebrews 11:35, Acts 20:10, Acts 9:36-41, and other accounts.
5. Acts 10:9-16.
6. Luke 3:22.
7. The life of Noah is found in Genesis 6–9.
8. Genesis 15:5.
9. Genesis 22.
10. Genesis 22:8.
11. Matthew 18:15–17.
12. 2 Samuel 12:7.
13. Galatians 2:11.
14. Revelation 19:15.
15. Numbers 1–3.

16. Deuteronomy 12:8.
17. 1 Samuel 17.
18. 1 Timothy 4:1.
19. Matthew 10:19,20.
20. Hebrews 11:38.
21. Psalm 46:10, KJV.
22. Mark 6:31.

Chapter 5

1. Galatians 4:4.
2. Luke 1:26,27.
3. Isaiah 7:14; Jeremiah 33:15.
4. Luke 1:28,29.
5. Luke 1:30-33.
6. Acts 10:1,2; 22.
7. James 2:20.
8. Luke 1:34,35.
9. Luke 1:37.
10. Luke 1:38.
11. Luke 1:31,32.
12. Timothy Ware, *The Orthodox Church* (New York: Penguin Books, 1963).
13. Luke 1:42,43 (italics mine).
14. Luke 1:28.
15. Ware, *op. cit.*, pp. 261, 262 (italics his).
16. John 2:5.

Chapter 6

1. 2 Timothy 2:21.
2. 1 Peter 2:1.
3. James 3:2.
4. 1 Corinthians 6:15.
5. 2 Peter 1:3,4.
6. *The Nicene Creed*, A.D. 325.
7. A famous saying of John of Damascus.
8. Jon E. Braun, *It Ain't Gonna Reign No More* (Nashville: Thomas Nelson Publishers, 1978), pp. 123, 124.
9. Hebrews 5:8.
10. Hebrews 4:15.
11. Ephesians 4:9,10.
12. John 1:18.
13. 1 Timothy 2:5.
14. Isaiah 26:3,4, KJV.
15. 1 Corinthians 2:16.
16. 2 Corinthians 10:5.
17. Luke 22:42.
18. 2 Peter 1:20.
19. Genesis 3:1, KJV (italics mine).

20. Genesis 3:12 (italics mine).
21. Genesis 3:13 (italics mine).
22. Romans 8:16.
23. 1 Corinthians 12:2.
24. Ephesians 2:2.
25. Romans 6:11.
26. Romans 8:32.

Chapter 7

1. Romans 12:5.
2. 1 Peter 2:9.
3. 1 Corinthians 14:37.
4. 2 Thessalonians 3:14.
5. Matthew 6:33, KJV.
6. 2 Peter 1:20.
7. Acts 1:20, KJV.

Chapter 8

1. Ephesians 4:4-6.
2. Bettenson, *Later Fathers*, pp. 44,45.
3. Jack N. Sparks, ed., *The Apostolic Fathers* (Nashville: Thomas Nelson Publishers, 1978), p. 313.
4. Luke 3:21,22.
5. Acts 2:38.
6. John 3:5.
7. Romans 6:4.
8. John 20:23.
9. John 15:16.
10. Acts 8:12.
11. Acts 8:14-17.
12. Acts 10:43-47.
13. Acts 11:18.
14. Colossians 2:8.
15. 2 Thessalonians 2:15 (italics mine).
16. Acts 19:1-6.
17. Matthew 28:19,20.
18. Romans 6:4.

Chapter 9

1. St. Justin Martyr, *The Fathers of the Church,* Vol. 6 (New York: Christian Heritage, Inc., 1948), pp. 104-105.
2. Matthew 24:15.
3. Matthew 18:19.
4. Exodus 17:8-13.
5. Luke 24:49-51.
6. 1 Timothy 2:8.
7. Romans 16:16; 2 Corinthians 13:12; 1 Thessalonians 5:26; 1 Peter 5:14.

167

8. Cyril of Jerusalem, *Mystigogical Catechesis*, Vol. 3, St. Cyril of Jerusalem Lectures on Christian Sacraments, F. L. Cross, ed. (Crestwood, New York: St. Vladimir's Seminary Press, 1977), p. 72.
9. 1 Corinthians 11:30.
10. 2 Timothy 3:5.
11. 1 Corinthians 14:40.

Chapter 10

1. 1 Corinthians 11:27,28.
2. Hebrews 9:6-8.
3. Matthew 27:51; Mark 15:38; Luke 23:45.
4. Hebrews 9:12.
5. Hebrews 9:24.
6. Hebrews 10:19-22. (italics mine).
7. Hebrews 12:22-24.
8. Luke 22:19,20.
9. Psalm 34:8.
10. Luke 22:19,20.
11. Isaiah 55:9.
12. John 3:3.
13. John 6:53 (italics mine).
14. John 6:55.
15. John 6:63.
16. Hebrews 12:22-24.
17. John 17:1.
18. Psalm 103:12.
19. 1 Corinthians 10:16,17.
20. 1 Corinthians 11:26.

Chapter 11

1. Edward B. Pusey, tr., *Confessions of St. Augustine* (New York: Random House, 1949), p. 207.
2. Romans 7:23.
3. 1 Corinthians 3:9.
4. See James 2:18.
5. Philippians 2:12,13.
6. Philippians 4:13.
7. Revelation 3:20.
8. John 15:1-5.

Chapter 12

1. Revelation 21:10-19.
2. Matthew 16:18 (italics mine).
3. John 14:2 (italics mine).
4. 1 Peter 2:5 (italics mine).
5. Ephesians 2:19-21 (italics mine).
6. Ephesians 4:15,16 (italics mine).
7. Revelation 1:4 (italics mine).
8. Haggai 1:2-6.
9. Haggai 1:8-10.

BIBLIOGRAPHY

Athanasius. *On the Incarnation*. Crestwood, New York: St. Vladimir's Seminary Press, 1944.

Ballew, Dick. *Coming in from the Cold*. Mt. Hermon, California: Conciliar Press, n.d.

Bettenson, Henry, tr. *The Early Christian Fathers*. London: Oxford University Press, 1956.

Bettenson, Henry, ed. and tr. *The Later Christian Fathers*. London: Oxford University Press, 1970.

Bloesch, Donald G. and Webber, Robert. *The Orthodox Evangelicals*. Nashville: Thomas Nelson, 1978.

Bouyer, Louis, *Eucharist*. Notre Dame: University of Notre Dame Press, 1968.

Braun, Jon E. *It Ain't Gonna Reign No More*. Nashville: Thomas Nelson, 1978.

Braun, Jon E. *Whatever Happened to Hell*. Nashville: Thomas Nelson, 1979

Cabasilas, Nicholas. *The Life in Christ*. Crestwood, New York: St. Vladimir's Seminary Press, 1974.

Cyril of Jerusalem. *Mystigogical Catechesis*. Vol. 3. Edited by F. L. Cross. Crestwood, New York: St. Vladimir's Seminary Press, 1977.

Dix, Dom Gregory. *The Shape of the Liturgy*. London: Daire Press, Adam and Charles Black, 1945.

Ellul, Jacques. *The Presence of the Kingdom*. New York: The Seabury Press, 1967.

Hoke, Donald E., ed. *Evangelicals Face the Future*. South Pasadena, California: William Carey Library, 1978.

Howard, Thomas. *Splendory in the Ordinary*. Wheaton, Illinois: Tyndale House, 1976.

Martyr, St. Justin. *The Fathers of the Church*. Vol. 6. New York: Christian Heritage, Inc., 1948.

Pusey, Edward B., tr. *Confessions of St. Augustine*. New York: Random House, 1949.

Schmemann, Alexander. *For the Life of the World*. Crestwood, New York: St. Vladimir's Seminary Press, 1973.

Sparks, Jack, N., ed. *The Apostolic Fathers*. Nashville: Thomas Nelson, 1978.

Sparks, Jack N. *The Mindbenders*. Nashville: Thomas Nelson, 1977.

Ware, Timothy. *The Orthodox Church*. New York: Penguin Books, 1963.

Webber, Robert E. *Common Roots*. Grand Rapids: Zondervan, 1978.

Wirt, Sherwood E. *The Social Conscience of the Evangelical*. New York: Harper and Row, 1968.

INDEX
TO SCRIPTURE REFERENCES

172